WHAT IS YOUR NAME?

HOW TO GO FROM BEING UNCHAINED TO FINDING YOUR TRUE LOVE, HAPPINESS AND FREEDOM WITHIN

BARKE FARAJ

Copyright @2021 by Barke Faraj

All rights reserved. No part of this book may be reproduced in any form or by any electronic or mechanical means, including information storage and retrieval systems, without permission in writing from the publisher, except by reviewers, who may quote brief passages in a review.

This publication contains the opinions and ideas of its author. It is intended to provide helpful and informative material on the subjects addressed in the publication. The author and publisher specifically disclaim all responsibility for any liability, loss or risk, personal or otherwise, which is incurred as a consequence, directly or indirectly, of the use and application of any of the contents of this book.

WORKBOOK PRESS LLC
187 E Warm Springs Rd,
Suite B285, Las Vegas, NV 89119, USA

Website:	https://workbookpress.com/
Hotline:	1-888-818-4856
Email:	admin@workbookpress.com

Ordering Information:
Quantity sales. Special discounts are available on quantity purchases by corporations, associations, and others.
For details, contact the publisher at the address above.

Library of Congress Control Number:
ISBN-13:   978-1-956017-33-5 (Paperback Version)
           978-1-956017-34-2 (Digital Version)

REV. DATE: 18/08/2021

WHAT IS YOUR NAME?

How to Go from Being Unchained to Finding True Love, Happiness & Freedom Within.

By: Barke Faraj

DEDICATION

With the deepest gratitude, I wish to thank every person who has come into my life and inspired, touched, and illuminated me through his or her presence.

This book is dedicated to my beloved daughter Tahiya Haidar Kamuss. I had to be the best woman and mother, I can be, to ensure she grows up and becomes the great woman she was born to be.

"Never be bullied into silence. Never allow yourself to be made a victim. Accept no one's definition of your life, but define yourself."

-Harvey Fierstein

"You yourself, as much as anybody in the entire universe, deserve your Love and Affection"

-Buddha

FOREWORD

I was inspired by my mama's life as well as my sisters. This was borne from seeing them in poverty; not just about the lack of wealth, but the way women have been devalued and perceived as weak, worthless and hidden away.

To every woman in the world, who is suffering due to a lack of understanding, due to differing belief systems, culture/religions, status, education and environments. Women are underestimated by human kind. Women are so much more and, YES, they are more driven by their emotions. When a woman learns to master her relationship with herself, a woman can achieve anything she desires and can have everything and more; in her reality.

Life is for living not suffering, but only you can make that choice to live your life for you. You only get one chance to live your life, so let's make it on your own terms. We are given the most precious gift that is known to all human and that is Free Will:

- ▶ Freedom of choice
- ▶ Freedom to Love whomever we want
- ▶ Freedom to live the life we choose
- ▶ Freedom of wealth and health

RELATIONSHIP

The definition in the dictionary for relationship is:

"*Dependence, alliance, kinship. Affinity, Relationship, kinship referring to connection with others by blood or by marriage*". (dictionary.com)

The term relationship is applied to a connection either by birth or by marriage whereas Kinship generally denotes common descent and implies a more intimate connection over relationship bringing with it the ties and obligations.

This book is an in-depth look into the relationship with the self.

Why?

It all starts with you.

Now is the time in your life to be responsible, through reclaiming yourself in body, mind and spirit. Every woman has a story and my story will relate to yours or touch on what you are going through in your life.

Your name is your label/ brand and only you can associate with it in positive or negative way.

Start by saying your name out loud and begin to have that connection to your name. This will bring out the emotional side and allow you to be proud of who you are both inside and out.

In every chapter there will be something different for you to take away; self-help challenges and tasks which will be beneficial in developing and maintaining this new healthy relationship with yourself from the time you start reading this book; and useful for you to continue to maintain for life.

It does not matter what type of lifestyle you lead or what you are going through at this time. Regardless of who you are as a person or what colour you have on your skin or what background you come from? This book is for anyone who is willing to work on themselves for the better and who wishes to live in full abundance. My promise to you is that even if you resonate with one thing in this book it will be a bonus and a benefit and will bring the gift of having more understanding of yourself.

FOREWORD

This is the start of a new beginning for yourself. All I ask is for you to have an open mind, be ready to get to know yourself and find what it is that works for you and what your own individual boundaries are. For some of you who start reading this book and you are not sure of what talent or your greatness you have or not sure what skills you possess or not even sure what you have inside of you then hopefully you will be pleasantly surprised and see that it may be time to make some big changes in yourself and your lifestyle.

Welcome to meeting YOURSELF.

Now before we start, I need you to go and buy or make yourself a beautiful journal. This book will travel with you on the journey of self-discovery. Choose a book that you will cherish. Not a 99p book. DO NOT cheap yourself on this element. Get a book that you would give your best, best friend. Trust me on this. You will thank me later.

ACKNOWLEDGMENTS

"When you adopt the viewpoint that there is nothing that exists that is not part of you, that there is no one who exists who is not part of you, that any judgment you make is self-judgment, that any criticism you level is self-criticism, you will wisely extend to yourself an unconditional love that will be the light of the world."

-Harry Palmer

With the deepest gratitude I wish to thank every person who has come into my life and inspired, touched and illuminated me through their presence.

You will see me using words in Swahili or Arabic which was a respectful manner to call the elders. Some words that I used; -Grandma is Bibi in short Bi, Grandpa is Babu, Mother is mama in short ma, Father is Baba, Uncle on our father's side in Arab Ami (rather) than uncle, older sister is Dada, (Older Brother is Kaka but I do not have one),

I am so happy and grateful to have amazing role models: Grandma Bi Saida, Grandpa Babu, my Mama Hajra Hassan, my father Baba Faraj Ali Islam, grandma, uncle, my sisters- Dada Nuru, Ashura, Fteimun, Latifa, Farhat, Zahra, Maliha and my brothers Hassan and Hussain.

To the dearest people who came to my life in my journey of self- development and some became part of my family, Fatou Kassama Bayo, Safiya Mohammed, Warren Ryan, Karmin Mackael, Dilara Tetik, Faisal Khokhar, Latiika Russell.

To the father of my children who gave me the best gifts for the contributions on my journey which directed me to the creation of this book:

I am so grateful to you for my son who is as special as you are and who I gave my father's name to keep his memories alive Faraj Kamuss.

I also would like to thank the Organisations that supported me in my journey so far:

The Health Coach Institute

Parents Emotional First Aid

Fearless Academy

CONTENT

Chapter 1
A Relationship with Yourself 16

Chapter 2
What is Your Name? 22

Chapter 3
Being in the Present Moment 28

Chapter 4
What Does Your Reflection Say About You? 37

Chapter 5
See Through My Eyes! 45

Chapter 6
Reflect on Your Journey 56

Chapter 7
My purpose My Why 62

Chapter 8
Believing in the Process 72

Chapter 9
Fail Your Way to Success 85

Chapter 10
Law of Attraction (Law of Love) 92

Chapter 11
Power Within from the Source 105

Chapter 12
    Forgiveness is Power 113

Chapter 13
    Everything Weaves Together 118

Chapter 14
    Confidence is the New Sexy 124

CHAPTER 1
A RELATIONSHIP WITH YOURSELF

"To fall in Love with yourself is the first secret to happiness."

-Robert Morley

I used to think that by looking after others it was most rewarding; for me and for others. Every time I helped someone, I would get that feeling of being blessed, but then an empty feeling would come again. It was as though it was washing away all that good I had just done. This kept happening to me; I could not understand the feeling.

I did not realise why I was having it. So; I kept doing the same things, helping people, hoping I would get different results.

When someone needed my help, I would stop whatever I was doing and tell myself that I could come back to it later. Even if at that time I was extremely tired or if I was resting, I would tell myself that, because someone needed my help that they came first and they need me more. I would give them my time and my ear; without worry of them being judged, confident that no one would hear of their business or they had no fear of feeling exposed. My main aim was to leave the person high spirited and with some things to work on and resolve some of their issues.

In contrast I was the kind of a person who never liked to talk about my problems, or ask for help when I needed help. When I was hurt by something or someone, I would walk away if I could and if not, I would try to stay away; unless I could not, then I would suffer with it until something changed in itself.

I thought of myself as a patient person with unique abilities to find a resolution in any situation and in every person's lifestyle.

There's two parts in everything in our life and we have the choice and with that choice comes with a consequence. It all depends on what choices you choose from. One is good and another not so good.

My issues and my challenges have been that they have always seemed to put me in a place of sadness and as I did not like that place so much; I would say to myself that I would deal with it later using the excuse that someone else was in immediate need of me and so I would distract myself. I would work so hard with long hours so I would come home exhausted and just do, what I had to do then crash out and sleep til the next day and start again following the same routine. I got so comfortable at times in my job that I did not see time pass and years flew away from me, sometimes for a fleeting second, I was reminded of this feeling that I was meant to be doing something better and more fulfilling in my life. Yet as that feeling was inside my very core it kept asking. When? What type of life could that be? Why not now?

The feeling in my core felt like a fire burning inside of me which desired to be let out and do things for me. Without someone on top of me who rejecting my thoughts. But at that time I just didn't know where to start, all I had were these desires and dreams that I wanted. I knew I would have them one day; someday; eventually; as it was meant to be for me.

When I was feeling really down and low or when I had an argument with my husband or simply had a bad day at work or the hours got to me. I would take paper and pen and start writing my desired goals and I would always think and start my planning the future.

This future being when my children were 18 years old, they would be ready to leave for university then this would be the best time for me to start my journey I thought. And the first thing I really wanted was to divorce my husband.

As I looked at my life, I asked myself why I lived and shared a life with someone with whom there was no love and where I did not really feel loved in a healthy way. See my life for all the negative that surrounded me made me just to look past it for a while and seeing my life as it would be. It would be great to have my own business and that scare me to death as that would be such amazing life success. I would save money every month to ensure that it happened, I would buy my own home that had gardens to have BBQ's and summer parties with my family and friends. I would own my own car; I would close my eyes and see the life I desired and I would see my children and I would be happy.

I was on the floor in the kitchen planning, every time I was low or feeling overwhelmed with what life was like at that time or sometimes when my husband said to me that I was not a good enough mother or a good enough wife…

I was married at the age of 16 years, I did not finish school, I did not have many friends or know what my bra size was or dress size I was. I'm married a man who was older than me and with a higher education level and who had plenty of with family support. I already had an expectation from my husband before we were married that he would love me, care for me and support me no matter what

I wanted to do or be. In my belief system just because of his age and knowledge, I assumed he would be the man I desired and was ready to share with me a life time.

My promise to myself for my marriage was to give balance; by being equal in my relationship with my husband, by looking up to him and following the marriage vows which I did to my best knowledge. I could not understand why my husband was still not happy with me as I did not know what else to change about me and I cared so much `and wanted to make a difference in my marriage.

I started asking myself questions and reflect on our daily activities. I had to do some real soul searching and I had to find out where the problem was really coming from and work on it.

The Questions I asked.

Who has the problem in this relationship?

Am I growing in this relationship?

Is this relationship working for me?

When I started asking questions about my marriage and rating everything I did and felt. Then I was ready to see the truth in my marriage and I made the decision to walk away because I wanted to grow in this life and not to just to exist without my own dreams and achievements. I wanted to leave a legacy for my children and others like me. That is when my journey started. The journey of seeking myself and exploring those dreams and making changes that have had a big impact in my own life and the people around me.

Reflection

In order to maintain your journey for self-love and self-worth, continually reflect and appreciated who you are, embracing where you are born or come from, owning regardless what colour, religion or culture you are.

Challenge and task for you

▶ Take your journal and let us do some work.
▶ What does relationship mean to you?
▶ What role are you playing in your relationships generally?
▶ Are you growing in your relationships or just existing?

CHAPTER 2
WHAT IS YOUR NAME?

"If you don't love yourself, nobody will. Not only that, you won't be good at loving anyone else. Loving starts with the self."

-Wayne Dyer

Your name has a meaning and it has power. It makes you unique in who you are as a person. Imagine the amazing journey; from day one of the special sperm that won the race to get to that egg which started forming from a drop of blood to a fully-grown body with all your organs and limbs. From that day your space had been claimed and all you have to do now is to own who you are and walk proud.

Think about your own name and ask yourself these questions: What is your name? When someone is calling you how does it feel? How were you given that name? What does your name mean to you and what is the meaning of your name? Who gave you your name? Are you proud of your name?

When I was young, I didn't live with my parents as I was living with my grandparents in the city of Mombasa, Kibokoni in Kenya. There was a girl I used to know that lived in my area and her name was Habiba and all I wanted was HER name.

when I asked myself why I wanted her name so badly; it was because of the meaning of it and that is all. But guess what!!!

The meaning of Habiba is 'my beloved; Now that I am old enough to know why I wanted that name; I also know that it was because I wanted to be loved. Even though my grandmother Bi Saida would tell me frequently that she loved me and I knew she loved me, the love that I was seeking and wanted more than anything was from my parents. I thought at that time that I was not wanted, with a deep feeling of having been abandoned and I could not understand why I had been left with my grandparents.

My grandparents had had their own children young and they now had five grownup children who had left home. My Babu Said, was a safari guide which left my grandma alone most of the time. They wanted to help my parents; who had a growing family with a lot of children and perhaps still more to come; by looking after one of us. It was a logical solution. I was chosen. Not so logical for me. All I can remember is living with her. 'My Beloved Grandmother' Bi Saida.

I do not have any memories of my parents only those from pictures; although some days I would remember a shadow of my father coming to visit me.

I do remember my grandma Bi Saida, coming to the living room as I was watching television. She switched it off. When I asked her why as it was my free time; she sat down next to me and broke the news that would change everything in my life. That my father had died. A glimpse of his shadow as a strong man stood before me. I could not understand why he would die. At that time at my young age I did not know that he was a sick man and that he had been for a very long time; yet he was only 36 years old. I was 9.

My mother's image unlike the reappearing shadow of my

father was distinct but solitary. One single memory shaped and implanted on my memory like an image from a glossy magazine; clean shaven head; cut nails. I remembered her only at the funeral, she shaved her hair, cut her nails and was covered from head to toe. I remember asking why did she have to shave her hair? My mama's hair was so soft, jet black and sweepingly long because of her Indian bloodline. She appeared so sad as her skin looked grey rather than her usual fair skin. She wore all black from head to toe.

My questions regarding this solid image were answered almost immediately. I was explained to, that, they had to remove all her beauty so no one else would find her attractive in her newly widowed state. It made me feel sad and I did not pay attention at the time, hearing, that they all were going to Zanzibar after the funeral. A distance of over 600 km. I remember; I had a last look at my supposed sisters, my brother and an infant of just a few months old. My baby brother in my mama's hands. All I could think was, he will never remember our father at all. I said my final goodbyes; believing in my heart that I would never see them again. I felt glad that I was left alone with my 'this' Bibi Saida, as they were going to the 'strict' grandma, in Zanzibar. Really; I had more connection with my Baba than my Ma. Before the burial we were put in my parents living room where my Baba was lain covered in a white cloth from head to toe. Our Bibi; told us to pray for him and read the holy book, I remembered touching his head and praying for him and telling him that I loved him.

I disliked it when people called me 'the orphan' so I would get help. Some would genuinely feel sorry for me; but I was continually reminded that I had lost my father all over again; the wounds scabbing over, then being ripped to pour fresh blood.

My grandma Bi Saida, would treat me like her own child,

she taught me how to be elegant with my appearance and how to be a lady. She insisted that I had new clothes every fresh term at school. We had our own routine which was disrupted each time my Babu, returned.

The atmosphere changed; symbolised by the harsh hitting belted punishment. I did not look forward to my grandpa coming home; There were good times in my childhood but the bad times were present too.

I went to my grandma Bi Saida once and asked her if it was ok to change my name and she said "you have to ask your father as he gave you your name" I do not remember if I did or not, I just let it go. When I wanted to change my life for the better to ensure I and my children's happiness came first I had to take steps to ensure I got what I desired most.

One of those steps I took was to know who I am and that started with my name.

My name is Barke, my father gave me this name because his aunt's name was Barke, she was a special lady with a beautiful heart. She had passed away so he gave me her name to keep the beautiful memories of her alive. My name means Blessing. When I was in secondary school, I had an Arabic teacher and he used to call my name with such delicacy that I had to ask him "why are you calling me Barki" and he said "in Arabic there is no letter "E" and your name, it means Blessing so you have to call it with care and loving". As I was a teenager at the time, I just brushed it off but I have never forgotten what he told me. From the moment when I looked at myself and realised that I am a unique woman with an amazing name. The blessing I get every day from that. I share that blessing with anyone I come across with love and care.

My name has power and strength, with great Love and is full of blessing When someone calls my name I answer with such pride and value that is like I fall in love with my own name over again. I work hard so people never forget my name because of the experience I leave them with and the way I leave them feeling. My name is my brand, my business and my passion. I am whole as I am and the only changes I made is only for my own growth.

The life you have is a gift. The age you are right now is a gift.

Appreciate and acknowledge your age, where you are, what you do and what do you desire the most?

I did not always see things like this. Sometimes when I was working or when I was really young when someone called me by my whole name it scared me. It was as if I knew I was now in trouble or an indication that I had done something wrong. That was when I noticed that my name was being used for negative impact. But regardless when I choose me and see myself as person of value and worth so much more in life. I become unique, stronger, greater and it all starts with my name!

Challenge and task for you

- ▶ What is your name?
- ▶ Please write down your name in capital letters.
- ▶ What does your name mean to you? How do you feel about your name?
- ▶ When someone calls your name, what emotions do you have about your name?

Note: Write your answers in your journal. Write whatever you feel right now and do not worry about what you put. This journal and information are only for you and you can come back to it to add changes at any time.

Now you are beginning to get to know YOU. Please write down this three gratitude's and add your own, it is impossible to feel low when you are grateful.

I am happy and grateful to be alive.

I am so happy and grateful to me.

I am so happy and grateful to have an amazing love in myself

CHAPTER 3
BEING IN THE PRESENT MOMENT?

"One's dignity may be assaulted, vandalized and cruelly mocked, but it can never be taken away unless it is surrendered."

-Sir Edmund Hillary

The life we live in, it gets overwhelming at times with stress being on the rise. I live in London. Walking on the streets of London I observe the public in the early morning, afternoons and evening. Most people are rushing from A-B so that their physical bodies are present but their minds are not present. They appear to be like empty shells and if you bump into someone in this state you will hear "I'm sorry". These words which became a habit in utterance without acknowledgement of the meaning in it.

When I got my first job it was within the heart of the City of London. I was so excited to work there and grow in the company as that had been my target. For me going to work was like a holiday; as I got to meet new people, I loved being part of a team and I learnt everything there was to learn, so that I could grow and get promoted. I was told that if you are seen and heard; that when you show how hardworking, on time (early), flexible, reliable, honest, respectful, quick to learn and adaptable to new situations you are; you will be a great asset to have in any company and you will grow (be promoted) in the company.

That is what I stand for both in my professional duties and in my personal life. I am a great observer and it might take time sometimes to really know someone's agenda but I will undoubtedly find out at the end.

What I started to see in my job was that some people have two sides and employ a double face, as they will laugh with you and then stab you on the back, they would adopt favouritism, they were often nonprofessional, to the point of petty tantrums or other childish behaviour and they actual felt threatened by other people's ambition and success.

When I arrived in London, way back in 2000. I was so excited because I love languages and one of my favourite languages is English. I used to listen so closely so that I did not miss a word. I used to think they speak so fast and I had to pay attention to what they said or ask them to repeat it over again. I did not understand why in this country people liked to talk about their feelings all the time. It amazed me at times because I was the opposite of that, due to my upbringing and I used to think that it was a waste of time to talk about feelings as it is a weakness and that you should be strong and not share your weakness as people will use them against you.

I recall a time when at the age of 12 ½. I came off the boat from Kenya alone. I was nervous as I did not know what to expect and I did not know how long this trip was going to be. I came out of the boat seeing someone calling my name and as I looked, I saw a beautiful, fair skinned lady looking at me, smiling and I asked her who she was to me and she said to me "I am your mama". I could not believe it that she was my mama, it felt like it was the first time I had ever seen her and I could not stop staring at her on our way to the family home in suburb. I wanted to show her how I was so glad to be in her life, as I never thought I would see my mama and siblings again when they left for Zanzibar after the death of my baba at the age of 9. Now I had another chance to get to know her and my siblings. Being around her and loving her meant getting some of what I had missed in my younger years.

I was a new member to the house hold. I was a tom boy with short hair, who loved to wear suits and trousers and I felt different from everyone. From the way I thought, to the way I did even the very little things.

I observed everyone in my home and began learning about them. In the beginning it was so nice, but as time went by the novelty began to wane thin and I did not want to be there anymore. I wrote a letter to my grandma Bi Saida, asking, pleading for her to come and collect me and to forgive me if I had done something bad or if I offended her in anyway and for her to please take me back to Kenya. I handed this letter to my Ami, and promptly requested that he send it to her via the post. A reply never arrived. Despite my constant waiting and wondering. Finally, I despaired; coming to the conclusion that she too had abandoned me just like my parents had done previously. Twice abandoned; Clearly no one really wanted me. I could be shipped from pillar to post whenever it suited anyone and now, I truly felt worthless and unloved.

I watched my mama intently. Examining how she worked. Her arduous nature and her ability to look after every single person who resided in the house. Trust me that was a lot of people. I saw my mama work literally like a servant in order that she paid her dues and when I looked at my sisters, they were not helping her and did not care what was going on due to it being normal, the way people there treated others. This also came with an additional price that she had no voice on how to raise her own children. She had no money, no education and none of her own family to support her or her children.

My baba's side of the equation were the wealthy ones. They took charge of us by looking after us by physically supporting and housing us but it came with a great price. My mama resided with us under the wing of my Bibi. Remember, 'the strict one'.

My Bibi, had very traditional ways. My Baba's children numbered six girls and two boys including me. Her belief that resonated within the culture of the home was that girls were not worthy of schooling. They had no need for it so it was an incumbrance that was absolutely unnecessary. It stood to reason for her that girls would simply become house wives and look after their husbands. They would not bring anything financial to the family. That was not their responsibility. It was not the way. Boys on the other hand would keep the family name. They would be the leaders of the house. They were the ones who would need to be raised, trained and shown how to provide for their families. They needed the skills and education to do this and so it was the better option to invest in boys rather than girls.

In what appeared to be a slight contradiction to this notion, it was my grandma Bibi, who was the queen of the house. whatever she said came to effect. My Ami her son; was in Saudi Arabia and he was the one who sent money to look after us financially. My Ami, would ensure that there was food in the house. That everyone had clothes and he took care of anything else that we needed. My Bibi, was different from the sweet little granny I always remember being depicted in the picture books. Somehow, she would manage to create chaos in the house; orchestrating situations so that people; especially the children would be at loggerheads. Yet when two siblings would finally resort to fighting in the house, she immediately turned into a rescuer placing herself; slap bam; in the middle to calm the situation down. She would then relay all the goings on to my uncle by telephone and felt it necessary to explain to him that we the children were in fact horrible and rotten to the core.

She encouraged him to switch his financial support to his sister's children as we were a waste of his valuable money absolutely unworthy of his generosity due to our behaviour. She said it made more sense to help to look after his sister's children as there were more boys. This unashamedly brought a huge division in the family. An illustration of her internal mess making which unfortunately was extended to the outer perimeters. She somehow forgot to reflect on her part in raising my siblings; appearing to believe that they raised themselves and she was absolutely and completely oblivious to her role or participation in any of the situations that came about due to her meddling.

She told us initially and reminded my siblings often that it was their fault that our father died. Her rationale this time was that because there were so many of us; this was the reason he died due to high blood pressure. This was repeated over and over, all day and every day. The words sharply implanted in my mind. "You killed your father and now you want to kill me".

My grandma's manipulation continued when her other son my Ami was present. She would ignite my Ami by telling him that my eldest sister was bad or had done something that she should not have done. The first time I saw this happen with my own eyes it was like an awakening. My unrest was given evidence. I saw my Ami wait for my sister to arrive home. It was in the evening and the first I heard was the commotion of shouting. I then was horrified to discover that my uncle was actually hitting my Dada with a money belt. The type that the Arab's used to carry money with. It had metal running along the edge of it; so; something that would inflict a considerable amount of pain. She escaped his grip and ran to the toilet and shut the door. He pushed the door, but as he could not force it open, he left. I watched then as my Bibi arrived at the toilet door.

She told my Dada, that my uncle Ami, had gone and that it was safe for my sister to open the door and allow her to go in. I stood aghast as I watched, as a silent standby, unable to intervene; as once she had coerced her and my sister did open the door; my Bibi actually let my Ami, enter and again beat her.

I myself, hid under the bed; unable in reality to escape the chaos surrounding me that I despised so deeply. The internal pain rose as my shattered pictures of blissful childhood memories once again reduced. Again, reminded that my protector; my beloved; my Baba was gone. Now we had no one to turn to. An empty space stood only filled by his silent shadow that filtered into my memory. A reminder of my loss. A reminder of my helplessness. A reminder that not only could I not help myself but that I was powerless to stop the pain surrounding me. Yet in the huddle of the ball under the bed my adult-self arose within me. I was not going to be a victim or helpless.

In fact; from that day I made a resolve with myself; a promise, a determination that I would never have so many children so others could abuse or let people or anyone treat my children like that.

Within that ball huddled shaking I became angry, explosively angry. I was so mad; not at my Ami, but at my father Baba. Why did he have to have so many children so that he died so young. It was all his fault. Having internalised all the messages and voices gifted me by my grandma Bi Salma,

I promised myself; that me Barke, I would not have so many children like my Baba did. I would never have so many children that others could abuse and I would not let people or anyone treat my children like that. That day I hated my Bibi due to her action.

But what about my own mama. Seeing my mama powerless made me so sad. My feelings of protection surrounding her too. The need to stop all the injustice; all the hurt. It had to come; there had to be a way. My mama deserved so much more. So much better. All I wanted was to engulf her in a web of shelter. And so, I made another vow that day; that when I grew up, I would take her away from the life she was living and show her how important she was and how much she had a right to be loved and be treated like a Queen.

At that maturing age of mine is when I started to hate being a woman. Internalising all that I saw; worried I could turn out to be my mama. One who doesn't have means to look after her family. This made her weak in my eyes and I resented her for it. Perhaps making myself weak, women weak. I did not ever want to be or feel weak. I resented her inability to protect herself; I resented her inability to get up and change her reality.

Back in the land of Suburbia; I sat down in the kitchen thinking what am I living for in my life. I found that I was not happy at all. I had no friends. I reflected on my husband's life. I looked at him and put myself in his shoes. He had wanted a wife and he had asked his family to find him a wife. Things just did not work out that way. He had travelled to Zanzibar from London in order to get married; however; the young lady who had promised to marry him changed her mind at the last minute. His desire to be married stayed stagnant until he met his old school friend; my Ami. just by chance and he told him about the engagement that didn't work out.

My Ami said to him that he had plenty of eligible girls in his house and so he was brought back to the family home. My Ami selected me as the one to get married. He thought it would be a great match as my husband he knew to be a quiet man whilst I was always highly energetic. He thought we would balance each other and thought opposites attract He could not have been more wrong.

My Ami was living in a house next to our family home; the whole compound was surrounded by a 7ft wall and gate. My Ami had 5 girls and 1 boy and every sunset after the maghrib (sunset) prayer he would come back with his vespa. From the moment he entered the gates he would call all our names; me and my siblings; as if to do a role check. If someone was missing; he would ask where they were and if they had asked permission to be where they were. If they had not a beating was certain to be waiting for the person.

He was not so harsh on me; I had a different relationship with him. When I would go to ask him for money or if I needed something for school, he would give it to me. He made me feel different and special somehow. After my engagement he promptly applied for my passport and had all the documents ready before my wedding celebrations. I remember him driving with me on one of our many runs during the busy procedures and him telling me about my soon to be husband. He told me that he was a good man, and that he would look after me and he would put me back in school. After this reassurance he added a word of caution advising me that his weakness was that he was a drinker. Despite this; my Ami ascertained that I was in good hands as he came from an excellent family and therefore, I should trust in him.

Challenge and task for you

- ▶ Take your Journal and let's do some work.
- ▶ What did you tell yourself Internally?
- ▶ Write down the internal messages you gave yourself in these three stages of your life. Let us examine both the good and the not so good and see what makes you tick. Meaning what messages have you brought along with you on your amazing life journey.

  o Adolescent: - Positive- Negative

  o Youth: - Positive – Negative

  o Adult: - Positive – Negative

What messages did you receive Externally?

Now let us look at the messages that you were gifted with by others in these critical stages of your life. Try and write something down for each but it is ok if any of it causes too many difficult memories it is fine to take a break and re visit it when you are able.

  o Adolescent: - Positive – Negative

  o Youth: - Positive – Negative

  o Adult: - Positive – Negative

CHAPTER 4
WHAT DOES YOUR REFLECTION SAY ABOUT YOU!!!

"It is all about falling in love with yourself and sharing that love with someone who appreciates you, rather than looking for love to compensate for a self-love deficit."

-Eartha kitt

I found myself staring in a mirror, I forgot why I was in the toilet and for the first time in a long time it was like time had stopped for me. In my head I remember seeing myself as sixteen years old; when I got married with a size 8 dress on; then time moved forward and I could see myself in the present moment. What a surprise I got at the way I looked. I looked at myself from head to toe with tears coming out of my eyes. My Body, my image, my thoughts and my personality were now so different and I examined my sad drawn face. The veil had come away and I could see myself for who I was.

That night after 14 years of marriage I held the intense realisation of the darkness that surrounded me and everything else that came with it.

And as I looked at myself with horror; I could see in me that everything I was doing was to please all the people who crossed my path and this was in spite of the existence of all my responsibilities; my children, my husband, my in-laws. Overwhelmed by my culture, my religion and lifestyle I now asked as I looked "Where am I"? The I that made me individual, the I that made me special, the I that I knew I was at sixteen. Where was I?

I saw myself fat, long and sad face, a person with little to no energy, sexually deprived; and all these suppressed emotions which clearly had led to one outcome; depression. I was just an existence. What was going through my mind is what had been implanted from the person who was supposed to be my partner; supposed to be my lover and my friend all in one; my husband. Clearly; he was far from that. This man who had been given the honour of loving, caring for and supporting me and given the honour of seeing me blossom into a woman and baring his children. He had been given such opportunity which washed down the river like a rainstorm overwhelming its banks and destroying its vegetation. I had been lost somewhere along the way during the storm.

My arranged married at 16 years had given me little time to breath the air of adulthood. I ripened maturity; seemingly ready only for child birth. I immediately got pregnant within weeks of being married and after giving birth; God once again bestowed upon me the warm air of fertilisation and four months later I got pregnant again this time giving me a son. After that I had always to look for ways to save money. My natural state meant I would be a little savvy with money; spend a little save a little. I did not expect to work for my entire life and always kept an eye on the future so I would look for ways to invest believing it was better to find a way to make money work for me. The problem was I just did not know how. I knew one way was to own my own home as this gives freedom after it is paid off.

There was a chance for us to buy a house at this time. There was a key worker scheme; My husband was working as police personnel and so he was eligible to get on the scheme. I was so happy that he listened to me; with this being one of my goals. So, he applied for it and when the letter came through and he showed me, all I could see was the amount of £50,000.

At that time, it was a lot of money to think about. We started looking for our dream house and as I did not know England very well, I had no objections as to where in the country he wanted to live. I would live anywhere as long as were all together as a family. It was such a good investment; not simply for us but for the future of our children. This is why I wanted us to own our own home.

I did believe that I was the best wife for him and that I was a great mother. I would always support him in his ventures and did whatever it took to make his life easier so he did not have stress at home. He really worked hard for the family and I secretly hoped that he too would support me in the same manner when the time came for me to spread my wings in my dreams.

House hunting was taking us too long and I asked my brother in law for help and join us in our search for the ideal property. With the extra pair of hands on board I was finally able to see my dream begin to turn to reality. Eventually we found this beautiful home with a great garden, a spacious kitchen and I fell in love with the brick archway which led into the dining room. When we visited the house for the final time; we planned to come back the next day and put in an offer. That day on our way back I asked him where the letter was with the cheque that the government gave us for a deposit. My husband handed it to me and when I looked at it, I was shocked to silence. There was an expiry date at the bottom of the letter. With an absolute intense sickening in my stomach

I saw that the expiry date had passed by one week already. I then had the enormous and sad task of transmitting this information to him. I opened my mouth and slowly explained the news barely able to comprehend the full extent of my lost dream.

The words that he returned with after such a shock was like having a bucket of ice-cold water poured over my head and I felt my exposed heart split into tiny pieces. This was the moment I knew that this man whoever he was; was not my husband. He had never really loved or cared for me. I remember looking back to see my child laying asleep peacefully in the back seat of the car. On our way home I frantically kept asking myself where would I go, what would I do. Helpless as I did not have a job or family to help me. and that moment is when I started working on my plans and my dreams of a life without him.

The cruel joke played over and over in my mind relentlessly. But it was not a joke. "How can you think I wanted to buy a home with you, you have nothing to give, no job, no education you have nothing that I want" The worst part was that he had known all along.

After that incident, I could no longer look at my brother in law and I could only apologise for wasting both his time and money. Stripped at that moment not only of my dream, my love, my future but stripped of my dignity; my respect; and my honour.

Life changed almost immediately. These words were the catalyst for his emotional abuse. It was like a can of worms that he had opened but the worms just kept spilling out; those fowl words; awful words; berating me constantly. And because I didn't have a job and I had not finished school, I started to see myself as a failure in my marriage. A failure in motherhood with my children too.

I prayed for someone to come and take me away from my situation and make my life better but at that moment I had lost my value and even I could not see myself as worthy enough to get help. So, a new thought emerged, one that said that I deserved to suffer in this world and nothing good would ever happen to me and I had indeed become my nightmare I had become my mother. Oh; and how I wished so badly that it was not so.

I got numb; my body became so numb that I would hit my head after praying to see if I would feel anything. and would ask God why me? Why did he marry me?

Once I used a knife to open parts of my fingers and I stubbed myself between my fingers. The feelings would come on occasions and so sometimes I would want to stub myself to see if I would feel it.

What stopped me were my beliefs. I knew that I could not continue physically hurting myself as I would go to hell.

I wanted to keep my family together. I had no idea where to start or where to go and who to see. It was all so scary. At times I said to myself I would be alright as I saw myself as a warrior, stronger as if it did not affect me very much. I still managed the lifestyle I was living. He was not abusing me physically and I kept telling myself that at least I was safe. Yet it was excruciatingly unbearable at times especially when I tried to live by his conditions: I was not allowed to give people hugs; I am big hugger and it is my way of showing care and love to the person I am hugging. Laughing, also not allowed; and this made me feel like a dead zombie. If I forgot and laughed, my husband would sneer or say something bad.

Listening to music out loud in my own home not allowed until he left the house. Then we would have our own private party myself and the children would play loud music and we would dance, sing out loud let it all out until we would hear the keys in the door. We would instantaneously switch the music off and I would become depressed all over again. It felt like a black cloud covered the inside of my home. When I looked around the place, I realised that it was not mine. I felt like a guest as whatever he, my husband, wanted to do around the house or within his life that is what would happen. He would do as he wanted.

According to him I was not there to advise him. Rather only to have babies and be the wife he wanted me to be. To cook and to clean. When I had the courage to start voicing the things that I wanted; that is when everything started to crush and we clashed on everything in our marriage. Forced then, I had to ask myself why it was that I did not have the right to an opinion on anything and why my opinion was not heard or valued. I began to realise that this life was not my life rather his.

My husband was a surprisingly quiet man, when he was with people, he would like to show that he was a family man; kind and loving. He would give the best hospitality and was a wonderful host. He would feed someone and take them home and he would look after the children and nobody would know how he was when he was with me alone. I loved it when there were people around as I would cook and we would have these parties at the house often. It was nice to make others happy and it made him feel needed and I would get some peace as we would not fight. At these times we would only fight if it was about my sister; as she would call too much or turn up at times without planning.

Enough was Enough. It had been years of living like this thinking of myself as not good enough for anything and putting myself down. All this kept coming into my head. So much so that I could not maintain this way of life any longer.

The pit of my stomach was on fire; the fire that had been started when he shattered my heart. This fire ready now to tackle the unknown. The fear that was always holding me down was nowhere to be found. this time was the time that I could become my own hero. The tears that were streaming, pouring out of me and it was the tears which symbolised a new exultant transformation time for me.

I went to the kitchen and started planning and started to write about my strengths and weaknesses. I listed them.

Strength

- Love to Train New Skills and Quick to Learn
- I Love to Connect
- Socialise
- Open mind
- Risk taker
- Bubbly

Weaknesses

- No Higher Education
- Not safe in My Job
- Too Sociable
- A Huger
- Easily Trusting

At the time I could see a glimpse of my powers and strengths and it scared me so much that I underestimated my worth.

Challenge and task for you

- ▶ Take your journal and let us do wok.
- ▶ Write down your desired goal.
- ▶ Write down your strengths and weaknesses.
- ▶ Write down your idol or the person you want to be. Look at what type of attributes they have and look at yours and see if you see any similarities

CHAPTER 5
SEE THROUGH MY EYES!

"The most beautiful people we have known are those who have known defeat, known suffering, known struggle, known loss and have found their way out of the depths. These persons have an understanding of life that fills them with compassions, concern. Beautiful people do not just happen."

-Elizabeth Kubler-Ross

When my children started school part time; it was great to have time out and I started taking courses and also got involved in the school's mothers' group. One of them was a hand craft group. I loved it; after I dropped my children to school, I would go to Morpeth Secondary school for the group session which was 2 hours once a week. I really enjoyed it as I had people to talk to and I could choose whatever option I preferred. I learnt how to do embroidery and also learnt how to make a patchwork blanket. The first blanket I made I gave to my brother in law for the new arrival of his first child. When she was born, I was so proud of myself. It reminded me of my dad. He had once purchased sewing machines for each of his girls so that he ensured that we would have a way of making money later in life.

When I went to live in Zanzibar, I saw the machines and wanted to learn how to sew. It was really fun to learn. But when I found out that it was our father who had bought them for us, I immediately began to detest even the idea of sewing.

I did not ever want to sew again. I didn't see it as a good enough role for him to choose as a profession for his children. I saw it as a way of downgrading us girls. So, every time I set my eyes on a sewing machine, I would remember that my Baba bought one for us to have and make a living from it.

Later when I was old enough to understand that he was simply giving us a failsafe; I realised that his objective was to protect us regardless of what ever came in the future and my hate turned to gratitude.

I loved the class so much that I actually started sewing on the sewing machine. My negativity turned to joy. I created beautiful blankets, shopping bags, a door stopper, pillow cases, table cloths, table runners and plate mats; whatever I could dream up. It took the class three months to get complete everything; just in time for the scheme mentors to organise a pre-Christmas sale in an office building in the prestigious area of Canary Wharf. We sold nearly everything we had made. It was my first time ever to get paid for something I had made personally. When the £300 was slipped into my hands it felt like £3000. I was so excited that I couldn't wait to get home and show the money to my husband. I wanted him to be excited for me. To validate my achievement; so, I told him. Yet we cannot make people be what we want them to be. So, in spite of my warm enthusiasm when I returned home the response, I had wished for was not forthcoming.

For me; I had never asked my husband for money. I knew that he was working so hard for us so I always tried to ensure his life at home to be easy, so he could have peace of mind and get no hassle from me. Once in a while he would give me £20 and I would ensure only to buy something that I really needed and not to waste it.

Every time I went to enroll in a course in college, I would

stop midway as soon as it became difficult and even just the fear of failure would make me to give up. The memory of the fact that I did not finish school. I thought I would never be able to compare with my husband's education level and that meant I would not have or be able to get a good job. I would have to start from the beginning to learn before being able to develop my skills to gain better and higher-level roles within any company. I ensured that I gained at least the basic qualifications necessary to guarantee I had equivalent to GCSEs and trained whilst working; as I did my BTEC and Diploma; for a specific role in management.

My husband started to complain about everything being expensive and how we couldn't go out or have a holiday or when he would take us out to eat, he would complain so fervently about how much it cost him; it ruined the pleasure of the time we spent together. So, I would learn new recipes to cook at home rather than suggest going out; promising myself that when I did get a job, I would buy tickets to go for a holiday and would never let anyone pay or buy me anything again. Things were not for free and they always came with a price. This particular price I was no longer willing to pay.

I wanted to be a Police Community Officer because it would enable me to be the first person to be there when someone really needed help. I saw the job as an investment in myself. Doing what I loved and having the opportunity to grow within a company.

Secretly; I also thought that it would bring my husband closer to me and that he might understand me more with him working with the police too. Instead of his blessing; he decided to point out all the worst things that could happen if I became a police officer. He categorically said that he did not want me to do it; telling me I needed his approval and without it there would be no blessing in the job. This approval he ardently retained despite me trying to persuade him. I explained to him that I had to do it for us; in order for us to have a chance for a better lifestyle. I tried to go through the application process 4 times. However; each time I failed the rigorous tests I would get up and start the process again. By the time it came to the fifth time round I completed everything necessary all the way to the fitness section. In the middle of running around the last lap I literally stopped dead in my tracks. It hit me like a thunderbolt, all I was doing was trying to prove that I could do it to my husband. All the passion that I had had at the beginning was all gone. Whittled away little by little by his negative voice playing in my head. All that remained was his ego playing me. At that point there was only one thing left for me to do after such a realisation. I had to stop and walk away with a smile on my face.

After having gone to my fourth interview and waiting for an answer from the police, my husband continued to complain about the fact that he had to feed me and pay the bills by himself. The delivery of their refusal came. Even though I really wanted to do something meaningful in my life the very fact that he could not understand or agree with me on this; meant that the only thing to do was to get a temporary position and then go back to try again. So, I chose a job that would not challenge me and one I knew that I would get with little effort.

I am sure that the nagging voice from my husband had reduced enough so that the pressure that he had placed on me indirectly to earn my keep was no longer such an issue.

After one year of working I had accumulated a lot of overpaid tax. When they paid me back; I was able to pay for the tickets for us all to go back home; the only thing my husband needed was to have some spending money. My actual salary having been eaten by various commitments. I took over the payment of the rent and the rest was consumed by things like the children's school uniform or when his or my family needed something back home it became my responsibility to facilitate it. Such things meant that by the time the trip was paid for I did not have anything extra to facilitate spending money. None the less I was so happy that I was going back home. It had been 9 years since I left the country and I could not wait to see my family.

My husband promised that we would get our own apartment but that did not happen so we ended up staying at his family's house. The whole holiday was spent just visiting house after house. It was not how I had envisioned things. I didn't like it at all. I simply wanted to take my children to see the country; show them different things and allow them to explore Zanzibar's treasures through different activities. I am sure for some; meeting all sorts of extended family would be enjoyable; but for me no. I promised myself never to go on holiday with him again after what I experienced.

Coming back to London I made sure everything and everyone went back to the usual routine. I ensured the children went to school early then I would have to run to work and then I would need to come back before they finished school.

Sometimes, I would fall down whilst running or whilst going up the stairs; I was trying so hard to fit everything into my busy time slot. I would often miss my break to ensure I got paid and have enough time to get back to school in time to pick them up again.

I used to walk with my children even in the winter or on rainy days as I did not particularly like to take buses; it felt as if it was quicker to walk. The children at times would try hard to persuade me not to walk and when they started to understand more, they would tell me that it would be a really good idea for me to learn how to drive. With this encouragement I decided to start driving lessons. My enthusiasm short lived as my husband chose the driving school and I did not feel comfortable with my driving instructor. He was an older gentleman and as I have a tendency to respect my elders, I felt it imperative not to disrespect him by answering him back or being rude to him. Hence, he did not understand why I was unable to understand his instructions first time.

I felt unable to explain to him that I needed him to slow down and take things step by step. This translated into me once again feeling like a failure. If I made a mistake, he would call me a dodgy driver and I really did not like the way he makes me feel. One day I built up enough courage to tell my husband that I did not like the driving instructor. He being him; would say that the problem lay with me not the instructor. I persevered for one year and after having failed my test three times I finally changed my instructor. My heart chose a lady who came to our neighbourhood to teach the ladies near me. I took her number and called her. After a month with her I passed my driving test, I was so happy. Was I really the problem?

My husband put me on his car insurance. I was given a new-found freedom and autonomy. I started driving when I was doing the school runs; I would use the car to visit my sister or go to see my aunty or my in-laws. I would ensure that my children would go and visit their grandparents every Sunday. I knew how important it was to have family and so keeping those ties strong was important and even more so when they moved to Kent. It was great to have the freedom of moving around everywhere I needed to be.

When I had started working, I felt that I had the right to have a voice in my home because I was sharing the financial responsibilities. Even so he never wanted or did put my name on the bills; so, I handed the money to him to pay the rent; something that actually made me feel very uncomfortable. I am not a sit and take everything person though so I would question and challenge why this had to be the order of the day. But then he would challenge me by suggesting in that case that we split everything in half and clearly, I could not afford to do such a thing so once again I was silenced.

When I started to work, I was so happy to do things for myself as it was my dream to be independent and I was so excited and wouldn't ask for help or ask him to take me places I could do it for myself. This in itself led to negative consequences as my husband actually started to think that I was cheating on him. He would go through my emails, my phone bill and my bank statements even my oyster card statements. He wanted me to print these for him as he was paying for my phone bill when I didn't have a job. He would meticulously go through my mobile bill to see who I had been talking to; to the very extent as to check what time I got a call. I was so glad when I was able to pay for my phone bill and not have him question me. I thought that he was justified in this scrutiny whilst he was paying for it; that he had right to ask or go through it. Strange is the things human beings do and the things we expect and accept.

Once he took the children on a weekend camping with his rugby friends and I got real time off for the first time and I went to visit my sister.

A year later; after being held by such intense speculation; I had arranged to go out with a friend and she cancelled on me at the last minute. Rather than explain this to my husband I decided to throw caution to the wind and live a little as it were. I decided that I would go out by myself without telling him of the cancellation and go and enjoy my own company. I wanted to go out that night so I did. I had never gone out or done things without him knowing about, before I wanted to be daring and go by myself and I didn't want him to know about it as I knew it would start another argument. I am not the secretive type and after his usual questioning I could not keep t hidden. He was so happy that his suspicions were right but the accusations that followed went beyond human belief. Did this man really understand so little about me? His ludicrous suggestions were so demeaning and defamatory that any normal person would question his sanity or mine. He would accuse me of bringing men to our home and having sex whilst my children were in the flat. All this supposedly when he was working his night shifts. It puzzled me where would he get these ideas from and I would ask myself what happened to him in his past that made him think in such a manner. Who hurt him before to the point that he did not have any trust in me at all?

Once when he was sifting through my emails; he found one email I had sent to a man's name. It was a piece of course work that I was doing and there was nothing that indicated or said otherwise. That night he refused to let me sleep. Every time I would fall asleep, he would wake me and interrogate me again with the same questions over and over again. The next day I went to work exhausted and that is when I started to cry. I felt that I was at a breaking point.

I could not help myself for the first time I broke all my own boundaries; I told my Dada what had happened who in turn told my aunty and this became a big issue. They could not understand how such a thing could happen as they never heard of any such problems before and so were inclined not to believe me. I told my Dada never to break my trust again.

Christmas time came around once again and, in the industry I was working in; catering; it sees its busiest time. I had to go to work on the Saturday with my children to set up for a Christmas lunch which was set to take place on the Monday. It was also the time when my daughter needed to gain her work experience so the whole family was looking forward to an exciting day. My husband had planned to drive us to set up and then after he would go off to play rugby.

That was a great time for everybody, the children and I; we were so happy. We took lot of photos and the children had a chance to meet my manager's daughter. They had such an enjoyable time together. When we were finished; I called my husband to ask him if there was any food for the children when we got home. He sounded extremely low; almost depressed and he was not interested in what I was saying so I simply said that we would be home soon. When we arrived, he was sitting in the living room? I was so worried and was wondering what was going on. What could be the problem this time. After I came out of the toilet, he called me into the bedroom. He was acting strangely and then he told me what the problem was. He told me that whilst he had been cleaning he had found a condom. At this point he produced the item that had become his article of speculation and said that he would take it as evidence of what he had been accusing me of previously. He said that it was better that I confess the whole matter to him and that if I were to do so he would forgive me but all I had to do was to confess now. I looked at him in disbelief and said if I had used that condom I would remember.

I also stated the obvious; that had it have been used it would not be that clean. I could only come to the conclusion that he actually planted it himself to see my reaction. When he saw that my behaviour was not the way he expected to be he did something that I would never forget. Something unforgiveable; something that I could not forgive in my whole entire life. he called my daughter to the room, his daughter, my 14-year-old baby daughter. Her innocence stripped immaturely from her as her view of her daddy would be tarnished completely. He had the audacity to ask her if she brought a boy into our home to have sex with him. He then went on to show her his prize possession. I was so angry with him; she was only 14 years old and she was such a lovely girl to accuse her with this.

After that incident he started to demand sex any time and if I said no, he would have a tantrum or would start screaming and so I would have to say yes to him just so he did not wake up the children or make a big scene. At times it felt as if he was raping me because I did not want it, but he would say we are married so there no such thing.

That was enough for me and as I sat down on the sofa in the living room after a week or so of this trauma for the first time in my life there was no fear. It was a peaceful and calm decision that came inside of me. It was my turn to beckon him and I sat him in the living room and told him that we were done and I would never go back to him ever again. Granted he did not take my words lightly and he started to threatened me with the condom and other evidence he had supposedly been collecting over the years. His threats were falling on deaf ears. I knew that whatever the outcome; whatever he made other people believe; whatever he could try and get other people to decide; I didn't care one bit. I could not live with or be married to this man any longer. I did deserve more than this in my life and at my lowest point I realised that I was a strong woman as I was ready to be my own hero.

Challenge and task for you

▶ Take your journal and let us do wok.

▶ Use the mirror as your check in time for you by asking yourself about your day, remember to say how much you love yourself and forgive yourself.

▶ On a scale of 1-10; how much do you want to work on yourself, 1 is the lowest and 10 is the highest, where are you in this scale in yourself?

▶ What does your me time look like?

CHAPTER 6
REFLECT ON YOUR JOURNEY

"Living in a way that reflects one's values is not just about what you do, it is also about how you do things".

-Deborah Day

It was 2012. I began working for 12 to 16 hours a day. In reality; I was running away from home. I couldn't physically do so; I was scared of living by myself and most of all I was scared of breaking my marriage because of how much God hated such things. Things were not right I tried to change them; really, I did. It was so beyond my control yet desperation did not push me to anger God. I could not stand before Him and say that I was ungrateful and that I had had enough. So; I simply stayed out as much as possible.

My family; where were they? They were not with me. I tried; really I did. The dishonour; the shame. Especially my father's brothers; they threatened to disown me and that really scared me. Clearly; should I divorce it would leave me completely without the family blessing. Such fear; such anguish. Whichever way I twisted or I turned there was turmoil. In 2012; divorce was not an option.

When I was growing up, when we were out, we would sometimes come across someone sleeping rough or someone who appeared lost; I was told categorically that when a person does not have the family blessing there is a possibility that they could go crazy or lose their way in life and I certainly did not want that to happen to me.

In December 2014; there was a significant shift. This time my decision came from a deep inner place that was peaceful. A serene, gentle and calm place. A complete contrast to the anxiety and yearning of the years gone past. There was no more 'what if's', 'but's' or 'maybe's'. No more 'perhaps things will change'. No more of 'it is somehow my fault', no more pain, no more worry. Just a distance sadness and calm. Complete calm.

In retrospect I am sure the actual distance of time out of the house had already given me space to heal. The wounds no longer gaining an opportunity to completely be bombarded with fresh ones before the old ones had a chance to heal. No longer was there an opportunity for me not having the chance to breath. And in my breaths, slow and methodical over those two years whilst breathing in and out first in panic but slowly; after the respite of hours; in and out, reflecting and growing; I realised I had made peace with my family inside of myself. Truly, I understood that it was fine if my family did not stand with me in this matter. They were their own people; with their own opinions, thoughts and feelings and I had mine. And mine was just as important and valuable. My breathing in and out showed the clear understanding that in the whole scheme of things that they did not support me financially, emotionally or physically any longer. The blood ties were important and they were still very strong but that I had somehow in my now relaxed and deliberate breathing been able to let go. I released everything that was not giving me or serving my new purpose in my life; my happiness. At last I realised that my first duty was to my Lord and my Creator and then after that my responsibility was to take care of me. God created me, and I indeed was more important than the happiness of others. I had a duty of care to myself. And now I was ready to take it on.

It has been nearly a year since I filed for a divorce and I did it all by myself as I could not afford to pay for a lawyer so I went to the Citizen Advice Bureau for help and they were really helpful. The lady who helped me; the lawyer; I still remember her smile; her support; her understanding. Some people they make such an impact without ever even knowing. In my religion there is a tradition that says that a smile is a charity. And sometimes the warm gentle unknowing encouragement gained from another can change a whole consciousness. She helped me fill in the form. I wished I took details of that lawyer lady who helped me.

The second letter came through so when I went back to seek advice.

The lady who was volunteering that day was SOOO different. Obviously everyone has their own way but I felt her impoliteness penetrate my skin. Her impatient hurry to finish my turn meant that I actually had to ask if she would help me to fill the form. I studied this lady. Curiosity got the better of me. She was from the older generation and her smooth brownness having entered the UK from the Asian continent guaranteed that she like my elders were deserving of my respect. She did not know me. How could she. She did not know that her lack of courteousness at that moment and that point was as destructive as any villain sharpening a blade in front of its victim. Was it really intended for me? After making my initial excuses for her; my automatic; child reaction. I listened as she berated me "You should have paid a lawyer to do this." I snapped

The dagger that she held regardless of intention was one she had no right to hold.

I stood up. Stood tall and drowned her words into nothingness. I would find someone else. "Bullying", I said was not what was accepted or expected from The Citizens Advice Bureau. They were there to serve the needs of the community.

I did not allow myself to break the bounds of decorum; what I snapped were not my nerves, not my boundaries; but the chains and shackles of my upbringing. Knowing that etiquettes were there for people who were deserving of them. I spoke up to her and let the management know about what had happened. Her unprofessional manner had resulted in her not filling my form correctly and so it was returned twice to me.

I returned back to the Citizen Advice Bureau but they were unable to rectify the damage. I was in tears. There was nothing left, I did not know what, or who could help me so I simply walked away.

A few days later after mentioning it to someone at work; she offered to take a look. She was not a family lawyer but her critical way of thinking meant that within an instant she was able to see what it was the Family Court had needed. Like putting a plug in a tiny hole in a ship she showed me that they had wanted me to place a bracket in red pen on the Divorce part of the questionnaire due to all the delays. And so, the issue was solved.

I have been sleeping on my children's bedroom floor for over six months. I had to make changes so my soon to be ex-husband would know the seriousness of the matter taking place. Unfortunately, every time I would smile or talk and laugh, he would confuse himself into thinking that I had changed my mind and that it was an indication that I wanted to go back to him. Most nights, at this time, he would come home drunk and come to the children's bedroom where I was sleeping. His normal blurb of verbal abuse would spill as if saliva from his mouth, salivating on any hint of concern from me.

My only worry; always; the children. Hearing or seeing him in that state. He would be pass by or sit on one of the children's beds. I would be scared he could drop on top of one them whilst they were sleeping. All the while he was spilling his violence from his mouth; I would record him secretly; on my mobile just in case if I had to use it in court or let him listen to himself to show him what he was doing to his own family and himself...

Family: what is it really? My struggle now external pushing me to really be the hero of my story. Each hero shines as they overcome each challenge. The challenges and battles won internally now were being forced to the surface as the reshuffle of my life began. All management books will tell you that change always brings a certain amount of chaos and conflict. Individuals often refusing to stop the status quo. But I had made promises. So many promises I had made. To be self-sufficient, self-reliant to love and care for myself. It was time to fulfil all my promises come what may.

Challenge and task for you

▶ Take your journal and let us do wok.

▶ Create a list of Personal Rights as an individual. These you can acknowledge and regularly remind yourself of.

▶ Here is a suggested list to help you start off:
I have the right to ask others to help me
I have the right for 'Me' Time and for that time to be guilt free
I have the right to say No without feeling guilty

CHAPTER 7
MY PURPOSE – MY WHY

"We are each gifted in a unique and important way. It is our privilege and our adventure to discover our own special light."

-Mary Dunbar

Two whole years before this, I had told my husband that I wanted a divorce. That I was not happy with our marriage. I was so scared that I was trembling and he called my family. He called them all; there was so much talk. He called my father's brothers and he told them that I had changed, somehow trying to shift the responsibility of the problems in our marriage away from him. He told them that they needed to talk to me and so I was summoned. As if before a court; the jury already biased by his pretrial words.

He had prepared them well; so well in fact that when I was able to tell them my side; how unhappy I was. They viewed me like a spoilt and whining child. Really what was my problem? Disgrace did not come from their family. But why did my thoughts revisit this again?

Because the struggle of the happiness of women in marriage goes beyond just me. Beyond the walls of my house; beyond the screaming and belittling; beyond to the extension of the villages and the tribes as the cultures blend effervescently with religion telling us; All women; STAY whatever; BE HAPPY whatever; TAKE whatever.

When I was forced to talk to them, I told my uncles that I was not happy and their answer to me was "there's no such thing as happiness in this world" and "I have to go back to my husband and apologise to him" as "it is better to have someone rather than not have anyone". When that did not convince me the next round of trial was centred around why was I seeking such a preposterous thing: "was I seeing someone" if so, I should tell them or "was I drinking alcohol or taking drugs" and then came the finale, the ultimate, the punishment. If I kept thinking of divorce then I would be left alone without family ties and this is the one that broke my spirit, that broke my heart.

I was definitely ready to punish myself as I strongly believed my happiness would cost me something. I knew it would be hard for me and that it would going to be a difficult thing to forgive myself for but at the time I just blundered forward into the realms of the darkness that I was expecting. Doomed and destined to doom. I did not mind that much that I was to be hurt and damaged in the process as I saw myself of worthy of such fate. But my children, I needed them to be protected from the wrath of reality. My fate, in my understanding had long since been decided due to my lack of education; having no money with little experience of anything of value in life. But my children's future.... well that was the most paramount seal of my affection. They needed to be nurtured; blanketed; cocooned and sheltered from the harsh pains that I was about to experience. They therefore; I decided in my head; needed to stay with their father. He would of course; if I was not there to disturb him; turn His life around. Of course, he would not drink; of course, he would be better equipped to protect and look after them. He had a good solid source of income. And whilst my family were about to disown me; his would offer him their full support. So certain of the outcomes I banished myself to the painful experience of my own tormentor.

I packed my bags and prepared myself ready to leave my home and submit my children to his care. Then he asked me to sign off my children. He wanted what appeared to be a free reign; to dismiss my very existence blot it out; as though I were a mirage that would float away from his mind and out of the hearts of my children. He asked me to sign that I required not one penny from him; not then not ever. That I expected but he wanted me to sign away my life by signing away my children; completely; full custody; no rights. Who was I? Was I not the one who gave birth; who stayed all those lonely nights whilst he slept in a nocturnal wakefulness watching the sicknesses of my children as they come in one by one? Was I not the one who sheltered their sadness and wiped their tears through these precious early years; Was I not the one who cried with them for their own sadness as they grew in their journey; melted as they smiled or watched in awe as they took their first steps? Surely, I their mother could not turn my back and walk as if it were a day in the life of. My answer was No No... No... NO!

I started to look for a place to live. I would go out early in the morning before work and start my cold and lonely search. After visiting different places, I could see a pattern emerge. Every time I found a place It would become apparent that it was not safe enough for my children to even visit let alone stay overnight.

On observation the bubble in my head surrounding my delusion that that my husband would be the best primary care giver started to pop one by one. I started seeing my soon to be Ex-husband bring alcohol home and getting drunk. Earlier in our marriage we had forged an agreement when I found out that he would drink alcohol in his rugby club or with his friends.

As I could not stop him or change him; we agreed he would never bring alcohol home because of the children. He now broke that agreement and began not looking after or feeding the children until I came back from working; which was well into the late evening. I had been thinking that this man was more mature in age; more experienced; more stable; more responsible but the bubbles kept popping. POP POP POP. NOT RELIABLE; NOT RESPONSIBLE; NOT CARING.

My bubbles were so light that I wondered how had I managed to blow them and sustain them in my head. Little more than a twenty pence children's bubble tube. POP POP POP.

There I was thinking that I had left them with someone who was more experienced and well educated that it would make him be more responsible. But he wasn't and my children kept calling me when I was at work late or looking for places to rent. Earlier on in the marriage I never travelled far or went to places without him. I was not allowed to go anywhere with him. The automatic emotional response that I had was anxiety. It made me so scared of travelling to new places and living with strangers was even scarier. Finally; I conceded and the only thing that made sense was to stay in my marriage.

I wanted to make everyone happy; especially my children. When I talked to my children; I realised that they were very insecure and they were worried about me. It broke my heart to see them in such pain and I could not rely on my husband at that time to support our children. I succumbed; the only way forward was for me to stay in my marriage and keep the family unit together. Sacrificing my freedom; my happiness and my independence. Sadly; I could not see the strength in myself at that time.

At work I was not happy; I was promised a promotion but

the management started stalling. This went on for over a year and as I was already acting as a supervisor; it felt as if this was wasting my time. I kept thinking of how I would survive without this job. With a promotion it would be even better for us at home I could earn extra income that I could save and survive. I had this feeling; a burning desire deep down in my core that something else was meant for me in my life but I did not yet know what that was.

One evening after working till my usual late hour, I travelled my usual route going home on the tube. Next to me was a lady who looked nervous and asked me where the train was heading and if she was going the right way. We started talking and she invited me to an event; as I was hungry to find a new idea of making an income, I decided to take her up on the offer. Whilst waiting to get in I began looking around and I suddenly imagined myself hosting my own event although a picture perfect in my mind, I did not visualise exactly what type of event that would be.

I went to the event and my mind was blown away. This was Network Marketing; some would say pyramid scammers, but for me it opened my world and my mind. It was all about Wellness & Anti-Ageing and it was perfect timing. At the time the buzz word on the streets was Wellness. It was a perfect time for anyone to invest in it. By the end of the afternoon I had already visualized having my own beauty shop/ spa and was emphatically making people beautiful inside out.

I was hooked. My upline/ business partner Gabriella Welsh advised me to go to an event at the Excel for Networking and I was very happy to go. I got there very early before anyone else arrived so I could get a great seat in the front row. Even now I love to be in front of everything and to have a view with no distractions. I wanted to see everything as it was my first time at this event. I wanted to absorb everything.

There I was there sitting not too far from the stage waiting impatiently for the speakers to come and deliver their talks but when I looked all I saw was male speakers, I asked myself where were the female speakers. I stood up looked around me and I made a pledge to myself that I would speak in excel to empower others.

That day my passion was born.

This was my new reality and I immediately started making connections in the event and met some well-known speakers. My journey to self-development was awoken within me.

My happiness and freedom of choice is always strengthened for me through socialising. I chose to look for signups with different meetup groups that could benefit me in my new life and create new habits for me. I was genuinely worried about my self-esteem as I did not want to live in a life where I put myself last or let someone else take me for granted. So; in order to push forward I chose an innovative way to look for these meetups. I downloaded an app called meetup. My first meetup was about masculinity and femininity. I was worried about my next step in life; mainly in relation to who I would spend my life with.

Rather ironically on my way to the meetup I got lost and I was nearly about to give up, but something inside my inner self reflected about the pointless nature of such a course of action. After having come all the way and standing outside I laughed to myself. Was not my famous saying to my children "always be willing to try before walking away"?

I took a deep breath and I entered the room. I stood there amazed that the event had yet to start as everyone else had come late as well. I was happy to again make new connections and friendships. The room was filled with more women than men. In this age of gender equality and emphasis of gender identification I believed this session was going to be about Men and Women and the differences between them.

The surprise that I received when I learnt that Masculinity and femininity literally hold hands within each person; which changed my understanding of self dramatically. The inner shift that took place was so deep rooted that the gratitude that I send out to the organisers continues to flow daily. These two people whose names and images are cemented like statues on my mind; gave their time freely and filled the room with a genuine passion and concern. They listened continually to my seemingly never-ending questions whilst I discovered things like a fawn turning into a doe; without tiring of this new foundling.

Having taken on so much struggle and responsibility I was shown that I was more in my masculine state than in a feminine one. My underlying feeling that being feminine was weakness meant that I often pushed myself to be more masculine as I saw it as a way to be more dominant and a way to get the job done. In doing so I had lost an essential part of me. I wanted to redress the balance and learn ways in which to do this.

I registered with a women's support centre for weekly meetings and talked in a few places with other women who were going through or had been through similar or different relationships in their lives.

Some of the stories of abuse meant that I actually found myself supporting those other women; more than I did sharing my own story. I just listened without judgement and found myself praising and encouraging them when they related when they had done something great for themselves.

After exchanging numbers and getting connected on social media. A new world began to open its doors. The Feminine and Masculine group put me in touch with more powerful facets of my search for self in the form of The Fearless Speaking Academy.

A huge part of knowing your story; of understanding not only the good and the negative in each of such is about owning your story. For me that came from having the ability to share.

And in this moment of my deepest struggle; in this moment of such soulful unrest and turning inside out and upside down as I looked for my next stage; my next step; my next ocean to sail. In this moment God surround me with love concern and caring. I was shown in so many ways that I could validate; encourage and care. That I mattered. And then I received the blessing of having more really special people enter my life. My journey took me to be given two plinths on which to lean; to ensure that I did not falter and cave to defeat. Two friends; like-minded in nature; also, Muslim and African. Two lights to illuminate my path and share in my sparkle.

I now felt alive and my energy expanded like a sun shining so bright. My smiles and laughter flowed because it did not matter what life was like at home or what worries I had. I was surrounded by likeminded people and everything inside of me was buzzing with high energy.

My children are 'my why' Nurturing them and being their role model is what drives me to wake up every morning. It is my staple diet of gratitude. I feel thankful to be alive seeing them grow every day. Being their role model is vital but what is really the most important thing of all; is to show them that anything is possible in this life. For me this was the push that meant I had to stretch beyond limits and challenge myself to do better. By trying new exciting things out side of my comfort zone and by being adventurous in order to stretch my lifestyle resulted in me helping others be their own hero too.

From the 16-year-old who did not finish school, the one

who knew little about supporting herself financially. I had now become and am a person who is independent financially and gracefully centred with my masculine and feminine elements in balance. And now in my new beginning I am an empowerment speaker, an author and a coach and this is just a beginning.

Challenge and task for you

- ▶ Take your journal and let us do wok.
- ▶ Time for a date night in with yourself!!!
- ▶ If you love to cook, make your favourite food, a candle it dinner, (alternatively take yourself out or order a take home from your favourite restaurant). Put on your favourite dress and make up and equip yourself with a pen and paper.

This might seem strange or be difficult for those of you who are not used to their own company. But give it a go and saviour the novelty.

- ▶ After dinner, take a moment to ground yourself by taking a deep breath in and out and reconnect with the present you and then write down five things that you will do and follow it up.

Pick things that will make you laugh, feel good, have great energy and make you look forward to do it every time.

CHAPTER 8
BELIEVING IN THE PROCESS

"To be yourself in a world that is constantly trying to make you something else is the greatest accomplishment."

-Ralph Waldo Emerson

14 02 2017 Finally my ex-husband left the family home because he could not keep up with paying for everything by himself and because I finally got the strength to not feel pressured to help with the finances. I quit my job six months before. I became disenchanted and lost my passion for the catering industry. I had resolved to become a manager in catering and when I had achieved this I would walk away. After being demoted and working such long hours my physical body was depleted; tired and deenergised. Studying full time alongside was also strenuous especially as the course was advanced. I realised that full time really meant all my time and I could not continue to do both. I really wanted to pass my course so I that I could change my career and become a beauty therapist.

I always saw myself as a business woman and I was very excited. I was both hungry and scared as I want to be successful so I could help my family and other people around me. I have always known that I had multiple talents and wanted to be free at the same time to do a variety of things professionally to create multiple streams of income as passive income. I wanted to start things up then employ and partner with others to grow eventually.

I have always been looking for someone or a company that would teach me how to be the best business woman possible and whilst thinking what it would give me the freedom of time and the opportunity to pick my own hours of work. Becoming a beauty therapist was one of those talents I wanted to have as a means of healing others. In speaking, coaching and mentoring people I was able to enable people to have a relationship with the self both inside and out. I was so happy to do this particular course as I would become a qualified beautician and masseuse which would build my clientele and let me choose my hours of work and have more time with my family and other business ventures.

My ex-husband would say to me when I was working in catering that it was a rubbish job as it involved cleaning peoples waste after eating and now here, I was changing my career. His next taunt and concern were that I would be giving men 'happy ending massages'. It seemed funny that his negative stance was a great contrast to the glee he used to get from using the money I brought home. I did not let him make me feel bad. Clearly; I knew I was not doing anything horrible because I am not doing what he thought I was doing and these were his insecurities were not mine.

All I kept in focus was my target until I finished my course and I had passed. I signed up as a mobile therapist and began going to people's houses to give them treatments. It was so scary at times going to strange areas and into stranger houses. But I had to do it for the sake of surviving at the same time I could get work none stop for one week the next week. Yet the work in reality It was so inconsistent that I could not keep up with any of my regular payments. I really did not want to go back to work for someone else but I had no choice. I started to apply for jobs near me as I needed guaranteed money every month. I went for interviews and although I received an offer for a job the waiting period for a start date had gone over two months. I did not want to go to the jobcentre to claim jobseekers' benefits. Coupled with the fact that I thought I could get a call to start the work at any moment. I was stuck a situation that I did not want to be in and I did not know what to do.

When my husband finally left, I was living in a surreal world for a week or so. This fluid state left me thinking I was just dreaming or hallucinating the whole thing. From the very beginning of my final divorce request he was adamant that he would not leave. He persisted that the only way forward was for me to go. It was his house; I should leave and it didn't matter whether I took the children or not. I was the one who needed to get out, not him. After so much stress and pain; probably for both of us; I was the one brings catapulted constantly into turmoil. Emotional baggage is hard to shift. My thoughts cascading like a pack of cards one after the other. He didn't care if I took the children with me. How could a father be so cruel? Not loving me or not wanting me was one thing; but his children. I said I would not leave either as I went to housing association to ask if the housing people could help me and they said they could not get involved and make a decision it was up to each couple to decide who will go and who will stay.

In addition, the area I was living in meant that it would take time for us to get rehoused. There appeared to be a lot of people on the waiting list. I was told Women in my situation generally go to a women's refuge. This however was not an option offered to me as boys or men were not allowed. My son was no longer small so I had no attention but to stay and endure his presence.

So here I was in the midst of the haze of having my ex-husband finally leave. Two years of uncertainty. My divorce had been proclaimed by the English Court System back in the end of 2015 but my unbeknown ex-husband had decided I should be left in the dark about such matters and kept all correspondence hidden. It was only after one whole year of bewilderment did, I call to check what was happening.

Before I got to actually enjoy the moment, the peace of solitude and victory for my patience; I started getting mail about missed payments from the housing people. They were now threatening to take me to court. I was so scared to even breath; everything was on my shoulders and I had no one to ask for help. I being the kind of a person who likes to look at the situation and go head first into something and when things did not work, I would reassess the situation and go again. I went to the local housing department to discuss the situation. The rent arrears were nearly £2000 and every week they were going up. The thought kept racing through my head like the tube train I took to work. How could I pay such an insurmountable amount? My children needed to eat and there were other bills that I needed to pay.

Real insomnia set in. Worry and dread hung over me like a lead balloon weighting on my heart. I had kind of skipped a portion of my life. The one where you learn how to manage money and be financially responsible. From 16 and being married suddenly into this whirlwind of a marriage that tossed me up and down and threw me out here in my thirties, a single mum who had never fully held the reins of responsibility before. Now I had mouths to feed and a family back home looking to me to prop them up and take the edge of poverty of them. I had never had to manage a household and the pillows of debt kept mounting and chaining me to the bed with little to no relaxation. Terrified was an understatement. I had worked hard to get to this place; now I was here the unknown reality of what I had been sheltered from kept me calculating, thinking; figuring out and eventually dosing for 30 minutes here and there. The problem to solve was how was I going to clear the arrears and keep my home.

The answer; first I had to go to the job centre as I would not get help with my housing if I did not register with them. My pragmatic and practical side took over. I trotted down to the local job centre. With all the strength that I could muster I asked about the impending job and the scenario which would take place were they to call me to start work. They explained that they would stop any money they gave me the moment I started working.

I had seen it happen to my ex-husband before, he got a part job in the Olympics with the security company G4S; the jobcentre charged him near £1000 which was nearly the same amount he got paid and this is why I had not wanted to go near to that place. It was the 2012 London Olympics.

A year before my ex-husband was offered redundancy and I told him to take it so he could pay his debts; maybe go for a holiday or have another chance to buy a house. He never listened to me. It was like I was hitting a brick wall as my advice always hit on deaf ears. Each time I would tell him something offering good advice every time it would hurt but then I would go and berate myself for not learning my lesson and staying quiet. In this particular instance it was not until his Sergeant said to him that he had to take the redundancy; that what they were offering him was such a good deal; he was getting near £38,000 due to his length of service as police personnel. When he did finally take the money, I never saw a penny of it or heard any more about it. I only saw him being forever miserable and constantly complaining about money.

This grew my fear and angst about not wanting to lose our home so that I ensured we paid the bills. I had asked him again to transfer all the bills and rent to be taken from my account and I would pay for everything. He refused and said that the money had to go into his account and so yet again I was forced to do what I did not agree with and I ensured all my pay checks were transferred to his account for over a year. This had put me in a very bad place as far as my credit was concerned. It meant that I was always in the red and using my overdraft.

I hated to go to the job centre every two weeks to sign. The place was not welcoming at all. But I was there for support and I was in real need of it, so I had to swallow my pride and ask for help and see it through. Confident that when this ordeal was over, I would never go back there again.

The part of me which was stronger was saying that everything would be alright and that all I needed was to be patient. After six weeks of signing on at the job centre, I was glad to finally get support and was able to apply for housing benefit to help me with my rent. It was so hard at first as my ex-husband's name was still on both the voting system and the resident parking. I had to take his name out before they would help me and so it delayed my ability to reassure the housing association that they would get their money back. It meant that every week without fail I visited their housing office and spent time talking and pleading with them; showing them proof of my plans and steps that would get their money back. On leaving, they were never happy as for them they wanted their money to be paid the day before yesterday.

I couldn't sleep and when I passed out, I would wake up late at night crying so my children would not see me and I would pray to God to help me find the solution to all my problems. I believed that I could not ask for a loan because my credit score was really bad. I looked for something else. What else was there for me to sell and get cash. I found my jewellery sitting there doing nothing for me I did not wear them very often. They were replaceable so I thought why not and so I took my jewellery to the pawnbrokers; the ones my uncle bought me. He had bought me both silver and gold jewellery. The silver ones my grandma had taken them so I was left with my gold ones.

Also, my ex-husband had bought me a white gold engagement ring. The funny thing was when I got that valued; I was told that it was only worth £12. I laughed that day and paid for my arrears and I was happy for that fleeting moment. But then the bank contacted me as I had not paid for my credit card and I had gone over my overdraft limit.

There was no way out for me so they had to put me on the red list and after a couple of months without money coming in to my account; I began to be scared of the post coming and was careful whenever I heard a knock on the door. I was on edge at all times yet was desperate to gain control of my finances as it represented my independence. It was the first time in my life that I would not surrender until I learnt how to survive and have the independence and success that I was craving for. Deep down however; I was feeling overwhelmed, frustrated and a failure and I was really doubting myself and every decision I made.

I love that I always look for solutions; even at that time my mind was telling me to invest in something that would give me quick results. I had to try something, anything, so I joined trade markets and other places. Most of them were a waste of my money and I lost out but that I was willing to try to double or triple my money. In reality I actually lost more money than I made but it taught me a great lesson and that was not to try things when in a time of craziness, Desperation can be overwhelming at these times to the point that fear and the feeling of being trapped in a situation can take over. I wanted to control everything in my life as I was conditioned to work hard.

By this time; I had exhausted every possible physical action I could take to change my circumstances. I gave up the fight to control and said to myself "what will be will be" trust in God to see it through and guide me through all this chaos that I was under and that was the point when I surrendered to God fully.

The resignation was not a desperate one but one of wonder. How will things actually turn out. I trusted my Lord and in submission, I relaxed and watched and waited.

Before long I got a call about my credit history. The people who called said that they could help me and fix my credit score They also explained how they would show me how to come out of my debts at any time I could pay them off and could start a fresh or I could simply wait 5 years and my credit file would be clean again.

That took a lot of weight off my shoulders and I could breathe again and not worry or have the fear of being threatened with being taken to court or have the fear of becoming homeless. No longer did I worry about letters or picking up phone calls. Everything was finally in my name and now for the first time in my life I could say that I was fully independent. Don't get me wrong I did not have everything I wanted but I was the happiest person I could be and my children were so excited with the new venture that I was in. My new rule was that whatever I was going through, I would share it with my children so they knew about it.

We are honest in our home and when things are tight it is alright because great things are coming after that, but still we had to plan our finances and I had to ensure that there was food on the table and that meant going to market buy in bulk everything from fish, meat, chicken, vegetables and groceries and have a little money for a treat every month.

The treat would be, possibly that we would go out together or buy something fancy to enjoy together. One of my plans was to buy one thing for the home to decorate it so that it would change the way we wanted it to be. Painting was one thing but at least I had to do what was in my immediate power and that was to cleanse our home. It took me over two weeks but I did it and I was so pleased with the result.

It was not just a cleansing of the house but a cleansing of the mind. Releasing all the left-over cobwebs of destruction that were embedded in my state at home. The house was finally mine. Free of all clutter. I was content with my journey so far.

I had already taken my first biggest step and it was the scariest time of my life since I had decided to come out of my comfort zone. That word 'comfort zone' in my marriage I asked myself what was comfortable and the answers were the same. Being dependent on my husband financially, a warm home, a family unit and the good days when there were no arguments.

But yet within that comfort I was still walking on egg shells waiting for something to go wrong. So, I had to say it was like 50% of comfort in this zone, not real and total comfort. Then I asked myself another question "How long would I be satisfied with this comfort zone" everything that I felt or got from my comfort zone was only temporary and I had to be on guard at all times. Especially when that person who was supposed to love me, care for me and support you, believe in you and protect you and push you in to my greatness. That person was not there not even a scratch not in my marriage.

In my marriage it started with little comments here and there about my personality being too overwhelming for him. I laughed too much with everyone; for him; as far as he was concerned my effervescent personality trait was wrong. I should not do that. Then it was about the financial situation that we were in. I had to find a job and jobs he took on the task to list for me the jobs I would be able to do. They listed as either a cashier in a shop or a job working in schools. Whilst there was nothing wrong with such jobs, they did not represent who I was or even a part of me. Where was I in the story line he was creating. Clearly; I did not matter.

What I desired most to grow within a company or industry but he didn't want to listen to what I want or cared.

He bought me a Motorola phone back when that was the name of the mobile to have. At that time; I didn't have anyone to call; only him and my in laws, I got so excited and happy when I received this gift. I got excited when I received any gift from him, as this did not happen often. I wanted to keep it forever and look after it but after a few days of receiving the mobile gift he took it away from me and gave to his sister. I was puzzled by all of this and questioned myself as to why "why would he give me in the first place if he knew he will take it away from me?" I was puzzled by his action.

A few years later he bought me a Volvo car as I was learning to drive to help me pass my driving test. I was so happy and thinking that maybe he did care about me; maybe he did love me and that he did want to keep the family close. I wanted to keep the family close so that meant that I did whatever he demanded from me I lavished once again my attention on him. I would not wear loose clothing dresses in front of him and then not wear trousers or tight clothes when we were in family or social events. I tried not to be too friendly with people, even though all of these things he wanted me to do killed me inside and made me feel paralysed and depressed, but I tried.

Before a month went by and I had gotten used to my car he told me the bad news about my supposed car. He told me that he was taking it away to give to his father in Zanzibar. The same feeling that I had had when he took my Motorola phone away came back. They all came back, all those painful feelings. once again, I blamed myself for trusting him even for one second. How gullible was I? Could I really believe that he cared about me and wanted us to be together but deep down everything he did meant he was pushing me further away and making it so difficult for me at the same time.

His actions were pushing me away and his words blaming me that I was the one destroying our marriage and the only thing I had to do was take responsibility for myself, my actions, my personality, my future potential and happiness. These words did teach me to get things done for myself and not to wait or expect others to get things for me because I could only rely and watch over myself as nobody was going to value my worth other than myself.

One day I questioned him as a father why he was not taking responsibility. His bewildered answer was more bewildering he said why should he explain himself to 16 years old. At which point I had to say that I was not 16 but 30 years old. Somehow unbeknown to my then husband I had grown up and now I knew how to voice my opinion and stand up for me. I looked at my husband at that time and saw him for the first time as though he was suffering inside. It was not my job to heal or protect him that was for him to do and at the point all I could do for him was to forgive him, to appreciate him and to thank him for all the lessons he taught me and walk away from my past and into my present with no baggage or grudges. Just all Love, happiness and being content with everything else in between. My marriage was a great lesson that was preparing me for the life I desired more and the opportunity to shine bright like a diamond I was born to be.

Challenge and task for you

- ▶ Take your journal and let us do some work.
- ▶ Time to let go of what was and find peace in yourself by following the steps below.
- ▶ Write a letter to your younger you
- ▶ The person you are now
- ▶ The positives
- ▶ The pleasures
- ▶ The possibilities for the future
- ▶ How well you have done to get through what you went through
- ▶ What strengths have you pulled on
- ▶ What have you learnt in your childhood/adulthood that you could take into the future?

Note:

This is the best time to reflection and view feedback from people around you. People, Environment and Experiences teaches us who we are by pushing your limitation, patients and challenges all these are your barometer to keep you in check on your present and what to come as the English say "NIP IT IN THE BUD" at the earliest stage not when is too far gone.

CHAPTER 9
FAIL YOUR WAY TO SUCCESS

"Owning our story and loving ourselves through that process is the bravest thing that we'll ever do."

-*Alan Watts*

I stood up on the stage very excited to be speaking at the Excel in London. It was a year before when I knew I was born to empower others through public speaking and that was where I promised that I would speak at the same venue as I thought that there needed to be more women speakers. And here I was it had come true. I was speaking with the best speakers at the Best You Expo and I had a stand with my banner, business cards, flyers and chocolates to introduce my name clearly in the field of motivational speaking. I had my dear friends and coaches who had come to support and encourage me and I was so grateful to have them there: Joshua Lee Graham, Safiya Mohammed and Fatou Kassama Bayo and my son Faraj Kamuss who introduced me on the stage. The audience was amazing after I finished, I had the most amazing feedback from everybody and got connected with great people.

2 years on now a single mama and a self-made woman I am sitting here typing this book. This is my third attempt writing my story as it has been an emotional ride I sit here and

consider and why am I writing this book; who is going to read it and what do I want my book to really be about?

Who am I writing this book for? As I looked at the world there are a lot of women and young ladies suffering through self-infliction, environment, culture/religion, validation through others or on themselves. Some are not aware of why these things happen to them, some know exactly why they are happening but are scared or do not know, what, how or where to get support from. As you have read this much already you can see for yourself what I have experienced and you should know how you are feeling right now and whether you are still in the place of pain or if you are already free. None the less now you are stronger and more empowered to keep moving forward and there is no room to go backwards; only forward.

If you are still going through a tough time at this very moment and any of these words resonate with you or if I have missed one or two things out, please let me know!

Are you Feeling Trapped in your life? Do you have problems with lose of identity, Body image, Environment, Intimacy, Work, Education or Business/Entrepreneur?

Do you Lack of Confidence, are you overwhelmed, with lots of life challenges? Perhaps you have specific issues such as with your Body image, Weight issues, stress, Depress, Anxiety and lack of support from people close to you.

I help individuals from different parts of the globe to be their own hero and have the best relationships with themselves. Come and meet my clients and the people I have been fortunate to cross paths with by joining my online group page. Here you can gain support and network with likeminded people.

Contact information.

Website: www.barkebeyourownhero.com

e-mail: barkebeyourownhero@gmail.com

Facebook: www.facebook.com/barke.kamuss

I wanted independence so badly that it scared me to death. Now I have it and two full years of independence under my belt; with all its failures. Yes, it has been challenging, often crazy, worrying, with fear creeping in at times. But despite all these different emotions my favourite reality is I am free to make my own decisions, fall in love with anyone I choose to. I now choose to live the life that is able to empower other individuals on how to have a relationship with themselves in all of eight areas of an individual, 1- Relationships 2- Spirituality, 3- Health, 4- Finance, 5- Career/ Business, 6- joy, 7- education, 8- family. I share my experience when speaking. And as a trainer, mentor, author and coach of individual's needs.

Speaking is my greatness and my life purpose and it comes from within. I speak from the heart and let the words guide me. It is like magic and although sometimes it scares me; when I let go of the control and surrender from deep down inside of me it is as if my soul is speaking through me. The way I am able to make others feel and get value from what I am sharing; even when doing one to one; I would mention something that would touch a person so deeply and that person would say "funny that you mention that" and immediately the person would feel at ease and be open to talk about what is happening to them. This gift is so special to me that were it not for the simple fact that we as humans need money to live; I would do what I do for free; in fact, that is exactly what I did in the beginning.

I was willing to help people so much that I did not feel comfortable; I did not feel it my right to charge. Seeing others grow from where they were to where they wanted to be; the transformation they undergo to start their new life.

When we have a desire that is deeper than ourselves and scarier than life itself; some will tread the root of self-sabotage in their fear of failure or fear of success.

Self-sabotage comes in for varying reasons.

Firstly; because of the fear of success or failure

It is therefore important to own the greatness of helping others and to understand that standing as a leader has both positive and negative elements. You also have to ensure that as a role model to others you are aware of the responsibility that comes alongside.

Being bare and clearly exposed or vulnerable for all to see you and your strengths and weakness, does one thing. When you focus when concentrated on weakness and that leads to the fear of being judged which in turn affects your self-worth, self-esteem and your confidence. Having less knowledge or experience in a particular field, our brain is clever enough to conjure up stories around anything we focus on. So; when you focus on that weakness what happens is even more reasons are created to attach to the negative; hence the reason why you should never even try in the first place.

For me; I was like that when I did not know about self-development or have any self-belief. At that time; I saw myself as a victim and everybody else was at fault as they did this to me. Every time I look back at my life; this self-loathing or habit of blaming others was not serving any beneficial purpose for me; in fact, it only made me sadder and have lower self-esteem. That meant I would punish myself even more with a repetitive cycle of "Why did I allow it to happen to me"

So, my perspective changed and I was; because of my conscious awareness of myself; I was able to view life as in a balance scale. From then on, I looked at my life like a scale that had two sides not just one, or like a coin that has two sides. A balance; as in yin and yang; with the tails representing my past and heads representing my future. One side facing backwards the other facing forwards but both completely necessary to form the coin. Every person and everything have a choice. A choice of what you do and who you choose to be. A choice of how we view and experience things.

For me the choice came as an opportunity in my life and I had to ensure my decisions were based on my true happiness. A sense of being with people around me who value me and raised my vibration with loving and peace of mind.

Life started at the point. Living the best life, being able to notice what makes me happy.

With a smile on my face and happiness in my heart I am able to know that if I start to feel otherwise, I can stop what I am doing and assess the situation. This means that I can move on with my life and that this adaptability can be in any place of my life. This life style is the best for me as I am honest with my feelings, I connect my heart and my head together and this makes me stronger. Looking at my life before when I only made sure others around me were happy and when I did whatever it took to make them happy. This was not good for me at all and when I compare that to the present; I am living a healthier life with fulfilment, abundance and balanced. I would not say I am completely cured as at times I do question myself over and over again about my decisions; my expectations and the reality of life itself.

One thing that I will never do again in my life is lie to myself about either people I have relationship with or people around me. When I do something if there is no love or it does not give me any fulfilment, then I have to let it go without being sorry for my action. We live once in this life time so it is important to make it count.

Fear

We are born with two fears, fear of falling and fear of loud sounds. Every other fear that we have is taken from others or acquired it during childhood. These we have the option to keep or remove.

Eight years ago, I held the biggest fear that of losing my family. When I knew I had to get a divorce; the most painful part for me was to break my family as I loved the family unit and my in-laws so much, they meant so much to me.

I was on the tube after working late one night and I looked at my wedding ring that I ironically bought for myself with my then husband's money after the wedding. I don't like to wear rings on other fingers or necklaces. The only jewellery I like to use are earrings, bracelets and a wedding ring and because I had to take it off after my divorce this made me so sad. It made me wish that I had a husband who would love, care and connect spiritually, physically and emotionally with me and that I would be with for the rest of our lives.

I had to say goodbye to what I wanted to hold on too, our family unit was already broken even his family will always be his family I only borrowed them for a few years and part of the consequence of my decision and action was that I had to let them go. Fear is an illusion from our imagination, fear is false it just appearing real.

Challenge and task for you

Write down on your journal and this exercise will help to see how far you grow and becoming your own hero.

- ▶ I challenge you to write down all your fears and really look at them individual and ask yourself it is real or made up?
- ▶ Write down all your daily accomplishments and celebrate them even if small.

Note:

When you want to make a change in your behaviour, thoughts and feelings you have to replace with the positive or the better version of what you had before that is not working for you at the time, your past and or in your present moment.

It has been said (it can be backed by science) that it takes 21 days to form a new habit but we are human remember if you do not have a shower everyday what will happen to your hygiene. Think of your self-development therefore you have to work on yourself everyday to ensure your life success.

CHAPTER 10
LAW OF ATTRACTION
{LAW OF LOVE}

"Don't rely on someone else for your happiness and self-worth. Only you can be responsible for that. If you can't love and respect yourself -no one else will be able to make that happen. Accept who you are completely; the good and the bad and make changes as YOU see fit- not because you think someone else wants you to be different."

-Stacey Charter

It's 2016, after my divorce and we are in the same flat not talking with each other. I am feeling stuck, worried and all I want is to ensure my children are alright so I take them out every Sunday to the café. Our favourite place is Costa and then we walk by the River Thames and I give them time to ask me things and talk to me about whatever they need to; without worry of being shouted at or judged. I would always tell them the honest truth and ask them their own opinion or suggestions and we always start talking about the future plans or our desires.

I received notification that my 10 years' bond saving had matured and I had the choice to either have the money or continue with the saving plan. I decided that right then it offered the best opportunity for my children and myself to take a break. So, it was decided that I take them to meet my second mama/ grandma Bi Saida in Kenya.

After I left Zanzibar, my Bibi Saida did not come to get me again. I thought she abandoned me and I had been so upset to the point of anger that when she finally came to Zanzibar, I had to consciously put these feelings aside. I had to look after her and these were beautiful times. Imagine even she brought me my first bras before I even had developed in that area precious memories.

The thoughts that I had held so close counted so much at the time but I found out later on in my adulthood that my grandma Bi Saida was innocent and that she had not been given any choice in the matter. It was my Ami that made the decision for her to send me to Zanzibar and for me no to go back to Kenya. Since I left in 1997 until 2016; I had not returned to Kenya. I had not wanted to remember that part of my past or even question why she did not fight for me or why she did not want me back. I wanted so much to tell her that I did not want her to reject me even though deep down I knew she loved me.

The reason that I was able to make such a journey at this time was that my cousin had contacted me via Facebook. Obviously, such time had passed it meant that I needed actual proof that she was who she said she was. Before I left to go and live in Zanzibar my grandma Bi Saida's first born son had his new baby girl and every time someone took a photo I would pull a funny face; as deep down inside I wished that it was me. I wished like that baby I was with my parents. So, when my cousin Summaya sent me a photo of me holding her I clearly could not deny that it was me and be reminded of my life in Kenya with my grandma. I realised at that point that what she had done was far in the past and what good she did was far more than the negative part; as really she had become my second mama. She made me realise that I had still been holding a grudge in my chest for this amazing woman. This woman who had cherished me, nurtured me and cared for me without asking anything in return. She simply wanted me to be happy and that is when I made one of my notable promises to go back to Kenya to ask for her forgiveness and to say thank you to her. So here in 2016 was the best time as she would see her great grandchildren.

Our trip became a family holiday with my Dada's family coming along. We spent time in Tanzania Dar-er-Salam and then myself and my children continued to Zanzibar alone to visit my mother and my extended family. After this I then took my mother with me to Kenya to visit my Bibi Saida and my cousin Summaya; who had helped to heal me by repairing my relationship with Bi Saida of which I shall be eternally grateful to her for.

By the end of 2017; a year working as a spa therapist and a receptionist to balance my finances; I was exhausted. I had had to take on even more shifts as casual labour. I could choose whether to work less or more hours and that suited me well in the beginning. However, early on in 2017, massage in the Spa became extremely popular treatment and I found myself doing 7 and half hours of massages, five days a week. When I explained to the management that this was too much, they simply said that I could not put a cup on them and that we as workers always have a choice to stay or leave.

At this time, I was given an opportunity and was offered a full-time position. But by this point my physical body especially my hands had start to swell from the tips of my fingers, my knuckles and all the way up to my elbow. I had also contracted some form of dermatitis on the top of my hands due to the products that I had been using. And on top of this my left wrist was sprained.

After visiting a GP; when the pain had reached an unbearable level, I went to the A&E and every doctor that saw me said to me to stop working as a therapist. They told me that this would keep happening so it meant that I would need to change my career again. I was given a doctor's note to relieve me from my duties as a therapist but without losing my position. I thought that this was going to be acceptable and that I was going to be alright as I also did other work in the same place.

It was absolutely fine at first; but after two months I began to be questioned about my position and I was told that they wanted me to apply as a casual receptionist as I could no longer be a therapist.

They said I had a choice either; return to my original job as a therapist or stay in the position I was currently working in but only get leftover shifts. They explained that they were not obliged to support or care about my wellbeing even though I did get hurt on duty and that they were not willing to help me at all. So, when my manager asked if I would apply to become a casual receptionist and I said to her no, I was employed into both roles so why did I need to reapply for part of my position. This made no sense to me. When I was at work as a receptionist, I had the knowledge of treatments which meant that I was able to assist clients in a much wider way than someone without such skills. This automatically made me far more proactive and helpful to the company than a person with only receptionist skills.

The Head Manager appeared neither to like me or the way I worked so I was under no illusion that if I were to reapply for such a position, I would not get it. I may as well simply walk away rather than to give her a chance to deny me of the position and with that decision this made me to have no work for months.

My fear returned about how I was going to pay my bills and feed my children. But this time the fear was much less anxious and more like an underlying concern but as I was in peace with God and my beliefs, I knew that the tool of the law of attraction was working for me in a positive manner. This enabled me to stay positive in my thoughts, feelings and subsequently my action.

I had to go back to the job centre as my hands were badly damaged and could not work until they healed. I looked for a job centre near me; so, I was sent to a different job centre and my new work coach kept asking what I really wanted to do and what type of industry I wanted to work in. I was still learning about the speaking world and all I wanted was to hold group sessions and to teach people to be confident and be their own hero. So, bravely I told him and he then surprised me by suggesting that I actually work with him in the job centre as a volunteer helping the youth. Of course; I said yes!

After a month or so of not having a job; I still had not started working with the job centre; there was a process I needed to go through. The line manager needed to agree for me to join in as a coach.

When it started; I did get success stories and great feedback from this. I was able to get referrals and present myself as an authority in my field. Despite it only being twice a month; I was still able to do other work too. At the spa people wanted me to cover their shifts in the reception so I took their shifts until this became more frequent and I was so blessed that my job was now more secure. So, I started helping my own community and I created my own work books for the class that I was teaching. This gave me many success stories within the job centre and within many different communities within the U.K.

Barke Faraj

Early in October 2018, I received a message from Muhammed Ali from ZAFAYCO saying he had a project in Zanzibar, Tanzania for women and youths to be financial independent and to build their confidence. Now by this I was absolutely stunned, as this news resonated with my long-held vision to do a similar thing. The thing that always deterred me was money and I kept waiting until I had enough experience and knowledge to go back home to build better lives for the people who were going through what I went through in my life there or even worst.

After listening to everything Muhammed said; I began to say to myself that it did not matter what was happening in my life right at that moment I just had to go to Zanzibar and do this for people. I knew that they needed this more than I did. Here I was worried about paying my bills and so I decided not to put any other things on my list of things to do. The Zanzibar Project began to awaken something so deep inside of me and it was so real to who I am inside; I was always keen on helping women and the youth especially those who want to help themselves but get stuck in a box of their life and have no idea what kind of resources they actually already have inside of themselves.

I asked myself whether or not this was my vision and asked myself what was stopping me or slowing me down? The hunger for me to be in Zanzibar and support these, women became my first priority but I did not want to stop there as I wanted to create a Woman and Youth of Earth Foundation as a not for profit charity, so that I could help women and youth everywhere in the world. To start in Zanzibar; where my family roots where was so symbolic. It is a very important step to take on anyone's path or journey to be in a position to help your home before helping your neighbours.

I started to overthink about going to Zanzibar about the cost and I began worrying about everything else around me. I then started looking at the reasons why I needed to go in the first place. It was all about helping others to be able to live their life in a manner they deserve. This is what I stood for. This was my goal. This was my way to shine. This was me. And so, my fears and my worries simply faded into oblivion and once again I was free to believe in my vision and the purpose of my path and my journey.

I asked God to support me at every step of the way. I asked for me to get the cheapest ticket; for me to get my visa on time; to ensure my children were safe. I asked for the food to be enough. I asked that the children would be alright and I asked to travel with peace of mind. I put in place a plan B just in case they needed support or the food reduced too much or if they felt they needed me. I had a support system in place as my dear friends and sisters Fatou Kassama Bayo and Safiya Mohammed so that they would ensure that everything was alright until I came back. From that time, I made the decision things started to look up for me. And yes, I did get the cheapest flight tickets and the visa came in the same day and that lead me to get more contacts in Tanzania and to get a speaking gig and to further build connections with others. And I loved that everything was going so well and fitting together.

I am aligned with my purpose and I am so happy and grateful as I feel great where I am today sharing my knowledge and experience in my life to others who wants to create the life they deserve and be there for them in their journey every step of the way.

I have arrived in Zanzibar Tanzania for the conference project as a guest speaker and role model. I come from the same country and so the opportunity to be there for women and youth of the earth, seeing my family struggle with life challenges, gives me more drive to do what I do and be the best version of myself. By everyday planting of a seed for their future and showing them their own resources to use to better themselves I am able to fulfil my own purpose.

There was hiccup in the Zanzibar project as the event was supposed to be 4 days and it turned into 2 days. We had to ask for 1 extra day as we are looking for results and the only way for this to happen was to show what self-development is and how it can work for Zanzibari youth. We wanted to make it very simple for them and as it was their first ever event, we had to ensure that the women were able to understand how self-development would be a great asset in their own life and success. To create a hub for the Women in Zanzibar to be members of, would provide help, assistance and training both online and offline.

I met up with Solveng Olin Becher from Norway. We had a similar way of thinking and she does everything from her heart. I love that about her and thought that I will keep in contact with her for the Women of Earth Project as she been in different places where she helped from the ground up and she is a very inspirational person. I also met Galina Hartshorn and her son Alex from England; United Kingdom, Galina is the leader of Global Woman in Nottingham and turned up to support the Zanzibar Project by raising funds to help the women and Alex also helped everyone with IT; the women loved his lesson about social media and how they could use it within their business or profession.

I love the women I met. They are so hungry to learn and see what they can do to make their dreams come true. Life is ready for them and now it is just up to them and I love their enthusiasm and their charisma as they can see what can be possible for them and their future.

Event day 1 was magical seeing the women starting with shyness, with feelings of nervousness and curiosity all at the same time. By the afternoon they were so happy to share things about their goals and the desires that they have as well as share something about their limiting beliefs as well. I feel over joy and excitement and could not wait to share my knowledge and show them what they can achieve in their lives today and what can be possible for tomorrow for both themselves and for others.

I love seeing people grow dramatically. It is like a child who cannot help but to share their new discoveries and when they find something new that they did not know before there is a sparkle and a fun as their eyes are wide open; a momentous occasion, it is beautiful. I finished the day with half of my training programme and I am so pleased for everyone who played along in my role plays and other games. And those who expressed the fact that they couldn't wait for the next day for me to deliver the rest of it. I had a lot of great feedback from the participants and from other speakers too.

Event day 2, everyone who came were amazing and all ready for the second day. We started with a great start which was based on gratitude and one attaining habit, which they would start to implement in their life and would continue to work on by themselves to improve their lifestyles. I finished my day two session and finished up with a visualisation and that it was taken very well.

Event day 3 was Group Discussion Day. When I arrived, there was only a few people in the beginning. However; after about an hour later people started drippling in slowly and there ended up with nearly 30 people in the room. They all had great questions and were ready to gain more understanding on how they could share their new adventure with family, friends and the others around them. They wanted to be listened to and get as much advice from every mentors, speakers and coaches who had come from outside the country just to help and support them.

Again; I had a lot of great feedback from everyone around me and fantastic feedback online too.

To be who you are is key to your success. For people to know you and to trust you, you must be ready for anything as a leader. You might be thinking other people you are in charge of will step up, but when the time comes to show up, they are nowhere to be seen. So, stepping up and ensuring that everything goes smoothly is what leaders do!

I am learning about myself through this journey and what I can achieve in every step of the way. It seems that only great and quality humans who are meant to be with me; approach me and are whom I would be always be happy with and grateful for.

After the third day because we finished early, I went to my sister's house where I had prearranged to teach other women my programme there; "How to be confident and live the life they deserve". The place was full of my family mama Hajra, dada Ashura, Fteimun and my younger sister Latifa were all there with me on my events and my dada Ftaimun loved it so much that she had rounded up all the women in her neighbourhood and got them to come to her house so that I could teach them.

I was so glad to have received so much support from my family my sisters and my mama. It made me promise myself to work smarter and ensure my desired goals always be my reality. They deserved to be inspired and empowered by their fourth sibling and I understood that whatever I wished for does come true.

Teaching my programme on how to use the Law of Attraction in a self-development beginner work book, to different age groups of women with different educational experiences. One or two of them had undergraduate degrees whilst others had finished school early or simply quit for one reason or another. Here they were in the same room; all ready to learn with an open mind, listening to each and every individual about their desired dreams and goals. I always finish up with either a visualisation meditation exercise. One that helps to start their new life and manifest it.

The next day was Friday the 03.11.2018 and I was travelling to Dar Es Salam Tanzania by ferry I was going alone but driven by my purpose; knowing that people were waiting to hear me talk and see an international speaker. Here I was ready to meet these great people those who were eager to show up and were as curious about me as I was curious about them.

At this point I would like to thank Luscious who I met at the Tanzanian Embassy in UK who helped me to get my visa and connected me with the founder of Be Inspired Be Blessed Elly David, it was an honour to meet someone like him. A young man determined to give from the heart. After speaking to an amazing group of young people in Dar-e salaam we ate cake as it was someone's birthday. There was some lovely music to finish with and a car was waiting to pick me up. I also met an amazing lady who became my client and a friend for life Kusinga, she asked me to stay as she wanted me to speak in her family church as they would love to learn. She believed every woman needed it, but I sadly was unable to take up the invitation as I already had another meeting back in Zanzibar.

I went back to Zanzibar for another meeting which was with New Vision Consortium Trainers. This was Zanzibar's first ever company which was looking to start to train 60 women to become and work in the tourist industry in Zanzibar. They were amazing people and I am always keen to meet and work with people like them, my doors will always be open for people who love to grow and support others to do the same.

When I came back to London my head was buzzing with a desire to open my own foundation and then this amazing lady Caroline got in touch with me via LinkedIn and wanted to know how she herself could become financial independent. We met up for coffee and introduced ourselves to each other. After talking about my trip to

East Africa, I found with great surprise that Caroline knew people in Nigeria that supported women and young people and so I got connected with them in order to be able to work on projects together.

I Love what I do. I believe that gives me maximum fulfilment and that this is what I am supposed to be doing for the rest of my life. I get so excited and happy with everything in my life right now. It does not mean that this place I am in is a place where I would say I am done and I have reached my goals, no this is just a beginning for me.

Law of Attraction is simple, - ASK, BELIEVE AND RECEIVE

All you have to do is think of it as the Law of Love.

Time to reboot your vibration from that time when you wake up in the morning with a simple step. Close your eyes and breath deep breath in and out and concentrate on the things that are going well with you and in your life and add one more thing you want, everyday start with small things and see how different your life will start to show up for you.

Challenge and task for you

▶ Take your journal and let us do some work.

▶ What are you thinking about repeatedly daily?

▶ What are you focusing on?

▶ What are you listening to?

All these questions are to help you identify whether you are asking for positives or negatives.

Note:

Think carefully about your thoughts. They are like a boomerang so when you throw the thoughts out asking for something good you constantly think about it repeatedly; when you even begin to believe that it is yours already and that you deserve it and without a doubt that boomerang comes back and smacks you in the face and bam you have it. Exactly what you asked for. Now think about if the thing you keep sending out is negative asking for a negative or something that is not good for you and what you get from it.

CHAPTER 11
POWER WITHIN FROM THE SOURCE

"Love yourself enough to set boundaries. Your time and energy are precious. You get to choose how to treat you by deciding what you will and won't accept."

-Sri Sri Ravi Shankar

Looking back at my life from day one; from the time I was born; not living with my parents; living as an only child in my grandparent's house; I really experienced a huge contrast between Kenya and Zanzibar. In Kenya women can be leaders, workers and business ladies. They can be both successful and ambitious without having any social stigma.

From the age of 12 I went to live in Zanzibar and I saw the difference in the way people think. The experience I got in Zanzibar was the same from my family; especially my grandmother. She did not believe in women having an education. Women should get married and their lives would then belong to their husband and his family and nothing would come back to the women's family. I kept hearing this all the time. As a teenager growing up in Zanzibar seeing women were often treated like possessions, and for the sake of not being shamed by society, women should stay away from divorce. What happened as a consequence was that women were left in turmoil with some women suppressing their feelings as a survival tactic.

I felt that I was living in a place where most of the people were somehow brainwashed to the point of insanity. Had I not had my experience in Kenya to hold as a barometer, I too, would have held these views as normal. None the less, I thought I was the weird one. Now as an adult looking back; I understand my experiences and have enough of a much wider barometer through travelling and age to know that in fact despite my young age; I was the sane one there.

In Zanzibar, there was no one who was on my side. I had no friends and no one who could understand things from my perspective. So; I turned to my closest companion; God. Being alone and different does that to a person. It allows you to search beyond and above for solutions and when the answers cannot be found; the one thing left to do is pray.

My Bibi would always wake us up to pray early in the morning for the fajr (dawn) prayer and in the afternoons, she would always remind us to pray. When the proposition came for me to become engaged there was no way out. I had already thought to run away; but I knew anywhere I would go people knew my family and as I did not know enough about the country as a whole I decided that I could end up getting lost which would of course result in my Amie, searching for me and finding me; so I immediately gave up on such a preposterous idea. The conclusion I came to was that God could make miracles happen and that He would have a plan, a solution that was better than I could come up with. And so, I prayed.

My Relationship with God.

I was born a Muslim and as such I had to learn everything that were the basic tenements of my religion from a very young age. And so; my religion became a part of me. I simply followed whatever I was taught and did what I was required to do under the ever-watchful eyes of my Grandma Bi Saida. I did well in this as she was not strict with me; all she wanted me is to do was to learn and complete my five pillars well. The pillars of shahada (testimony); Salat (Prayer); Fasting; Zakat (charity)and Hajj (pilgrimage to Mecca)

When I lived in Zanzibar, I was able to see adult life for what it was. I watched people letting other people down. I watched people's weaknesses of backbiting; jealously; envy and even hatred. I watched as people used other people's love as a form of weakness allowing them to manipulate or control them. I watched favouritism in its most intense and explicit form raise its head in injustice. This was my observation of the others surrounding me. I came to realise that until you understood someone's motive or intention that their actions could not be judged properly.

This, again, kept me from forming close relations with those who would call me their friend. I was truly alone in the world. God became my hero; my friend. I did not have to worry about what

God's intentions for me were; I did not have to worry about being betrayed by Him as I did with people, as He was the almighty. The one who only wants good for me. The one who loves me more than I love my own self. God only wants what is best for me. So, I trusted in God and had faith that that trust would not be broken.

After the family arranged my engagement; despite me not

wanting to get married there was nothing I could physically do to change the situation. I hoped that perhaps God would intervene and so I would pray every prayer on time, five times a day; I would read and listen to the holy book; the Quran; and I would fast every Monday and Thursday. In order that my efforts would somehow make God to change my situation.

My Bibi seeing such efforts was so proud of me and according to her; I was the best granddaughter. She did not know my intention; my reasoning that was secret between me and my Lord. She was proud only for what she could see that I was doing, things that were pleasing in the eyes of God.

I understand now that God's plan is not necessarily our plan. And, that whatever I have been through has not meant that my prayers were not answered, on the contrary. God says, that He answers the call of every supplicant. But that, sometimes we as humans are yet to understand the bigger picture. I knew there was no way out of the marriage. I was only fifteen but the engagement had already taken place. I did not know at the time that there is no marriage in Islam without the willing consent of both parties; but like I said I was only 15. And so; I began to ask God that if I had to get married; let it be to someone who; whether it be this man I was engaged to or someone else, but that person be someone who would love me and care for me. He did not have to be rich. As long as he was honest and would be there for me; I promised that I would work hard within my marriage.

So, when I had gotten married to this man who had been promised me after a year of our engagement and years later after everything I experienced in my marriage; both the joy and the incredible pain.

After my divorce I knew that indeed my prayers had been answered. I knew that I would not be let down by my creator. The one who sustained and cherished me. The one who is most loving and most forbearing. I knew that God had allowed me the experience of this man not because through this man's weakness I felt pain. Not because he was a bad man but because I needed to have a barometer.

I needed to understand the differences. The difference in myself. The difference in others. I needed to have the knowledge consciously of what I deserved. Through this test of mine; this God given test I was able to learn. I was able to fulfil my promise to God; as we are the ones who often fail our promises; not God. I had the opportunity to work really hard in my marriage. I tried and really God knew I tried.

And so; when my divorce was finalised; I knew that in this respect I did get what I always wanted after all. I learnt about who I was; I travelled to different lands not in exploration of anything other than myself.

Indeed, God has a greater plan for our greater good. I have discovered resilience in myself that I never knew I had. Love and beauty that expound effervescently through my laugh. I have been given the joy of life and for this I am sincerely grateful.

God became my rescuer to my troubled needs; even though sometimes I don't see the answer to my prayers straight away. Sometimes it will take days sometimes months or on rare occasions years. But at the end I will know; just as writing this book was a part of my prayer; that although gave me a husband who did not love me, he gave me motherhood; empowering leadership skills and the desire; empathy and the ability to help others.

My faith was questioned by my husband. When he watched as a bystander to my relationship with my creator; his defence mechanism would set in. Perhaps he did not realise that he was doing it but words can often be hard to shift. He would ask me why I prayed; what had I done to seek the forgiveness of my Lord. Little by little day by day this continual jealously and lack of control over a part of me which he could not reach; meant that I slowly retracted into myself. I began to hide my prayer not wanting the words of my husband to taint or spoil the actions. I did not want to continually justify my actions. Did he not know that everything we do we need to seek forgiveness within it? We are not created perfect human beings. Each with our own weaknesses and insecurities. But how could I explain this to him when he was crying out not to justify my prayer but to own and control every part of me; as he was taught by his upbringing to do.

I began to wonder, how he was in fact following the same religion as me. This question in me messed me up. I not only began to not pray when he was around by hiding it from him, but it escalated in my hiding it from others.

People outside of Islam already had a negative perspective of my religion. The media continually portraying Islam as some form of terrorist organisation. These elements made it comfortable for me to not disclose my Islamic identity. Not to share my deep-felt beliefs with anyone else. I started to tell myself when it materialised and sustained itself in practise as me missing the odd prayer or two or joining my prayers whilst in my safe secluded environment, that it was ok. God would understand he knows my intention He knew why I was doing what I was doing. I was actually scared, because I saw in real live women wearing a headscarf being verbally abused. I watched on the news how some Muslims have been attacked violently and I definitely did not want that to happen to me or my children.

One day I sat down and searched deep within myself.

I reflected on everything in my life. Examined everything inch by inch; piece by piece and I saw how when I prayed; I felt such peace within myself. My spirit, my body and my soul felt whole and complete and I realised that prayer was good for me. I also realised that when I did not pray, I felt lost. I came to the stark reality that I was only using God during troubled times. When everything was going well; I would not pray or focus on my Lord.

Challenge and task for you

Write down on your journal and please do this daily to surrender yourself to your creator for protection, guidance and blessings for every everything for what is in your control and beyond.

- ▶ What do you believe in?
- ▶ When you focus on the one you believe in how does it make you feel?
- ▶ How much time do you spend with your creator?

CHAPTER 12
FORGIVENESS IS POWER

"To forgive is the highest, most beautiful form of love. In return, you will receive untold peace and happiness"

-Robert Muller

Last part of law of attraction is receiving and it has two parts that you have to do before you receive.

1- Letting go by forgiving

My journey has taken me to empower and inspire others who are going through some tough times in their lives and who are willing and ready to master the power within themselves. Thank you for coming along with me on my journey thus far and seeing yourself grow within it too.

Everyone who comes in to my life I see them as having a purpose; often to teach; often to gift me with great memories; but always for a reason for which I am thankful. The best way to have a successful life is to appreciate each and every bit of it and by having a conscious understanding that the fragile element that threads us all in unison is that we are all human.

Humans are not perfect; a person is born as an individual and has their own way of thinking and doing things. As you have been seeing, hearing, and feeling how I was feeling at each moment in time at various points in my journey. You have been witnessing the steps that I took to overcome my challenges and difficulties and the lessons I learnt from the people who closely surrounded me and lessons given to me from those who were less intertwined. Each experience offering me the opportunity to expand to grow and to become me.

Along this journey of mine I have learnt that everything is temporary.

People, money, material things and life; everything comes and goes.

The only thing that never changes is God as God is eternal.

Everything else simply evolves around; with you or without you. One of the biggest parts that makes up who I am today is my understanding that human beings by their nature can give or do only as much as they are capable of. To be honest everyone has limitations within and so when you remove the expectation away from others and focus on God and have faith in His ability and His power then you can become happy and content with your life. This frees the space to see that everything is working out for you and that you deserve every goodness life can give.

2- Letting go...

As a young child we look for guidance from our parents; in my case; my grandparents; both Bibi's even though they were so different from each other; they did the best for me in their own way. Bi Saida was there for my younger age and the lessons she gave me were to be independent, confident, and to see how I could be beautiful both inside and out. The love she gave me was priceless and I thank her for all her memories, happiness, experiences and love she showered in my direction.

Bibi came in to my life at the biggest most important time of my life as a teenager when I was getting ready for adulthood. My grandma Bibi may she rest in peace, taught me to be aware of people and not to pay too much attention to what they said but rather watch closely as to what they do and how they behave. My Bibi was brought up in different times than I was and she did what she knew; what was right according to her understanding and as such I can only forgive her for the harshness of her words as they were received and the things that she did that caused me heartache. I no longer take those things to heart as in retrospect I can see the benefits in my life now as an adult.

All of us as humans, have pages we wish we could rewrite in some way; we make mistakes; but it is often through these mistakes that we learn and we change; we grow. And often, it is in our deepest and most painful challenges that we actually see the best in ourselves.

Through these things I am able to teach; to empathise; to listen. Through these things I am able to show others that great things are possible. That each and every one of us; despite our weaknesses to shine and also to appreciate the good times too.

Letting go...

As for my parents. My Baba; may he rest in peace; and my mama; they had their own reasons for giving me away. With that I appreciate and am thankful in that it started my journey and made me who I am today. I forgive them both; although I neither know or can understand their reason for doing so; as in my understanding I needed the love and guidance from them; I am glad to have them as my parents and I will always love them and pray for them and I will always look after my mother as long as she is alive until the day I die.

And breath...

I am so happy and grateful to have everyone who came and are still coming into my life and I wish to ask for forgiveness from anyone who I have said or done something to that they may have found hurtful, offensive or distressing. I have become a person with a thick skin; but truly I know I have always had the strength but did not see my worth or my value until the day I claimed who I am. My worth and my value and my life is important and I was born for a reason and with a purpose.

On a daily basis people who take your energy away and just bring sadness in your life; you don't need to have them in your life. Letting go of these people and putting people around me who lift me up and energise me has helped me to choose my own reality. By doing every day I have become independent; able to be happy and live my life to the fullest that I can.

My daily affirmations are "I am the author of my own destiny", "I am responsible for my own happiness," "I am my own hero and always find solution in challenges," "I believe in myself," "I have the strength to succeed," and "I give and receive love each day".

Challenge and task for you

Write down in your journal every day.

Write an 'I am' statement. Make your own and add one every day. For example: -

- ▶ I am unique in my own way
- ▶ I am ......

CHAPTER 13
EVERYTHING WEAVES TOGETHER

"We are dangerous when we are not conscious of our responsibility for how we behave, think and feel."

-Marshal B. Rosenberg

When I started to understand about the Law of Attraction as it is talked about in the self-development world. The Law of Attraction or if you have read the book – 'The Secret' it is also termed the secret and this can be interpreted in different ways. So what follows is my understanding about the Law of attraction in self-development.

Part of the secret is that there are three (simple) steps.

Step 1: Ask (who/what do you ask for?) what you desire most or what goals you have.

Step 2 Believe (beliefs/ self-esteem) Beliefs come down to your almighty or your creator or if you believe in the universe as most of human kind we do believe that there is some higher power existential from us, that is there for us and this helps us to have faith in ourselves and supports our ability to believe that we can do it.

Believing you deserve all the goodness and greatness of this life, believing you deserve it all. This is the major part or the foundation of the law of attraction in self-development. Therefore, before going forward; practise every day to maintain your life success with full abundance.

Ask and Believe. Those two things or aspects of it brought me closer to how it works and all I could see, feel and think is so similar to what my religion adheres to. It is so important to have gratitude to God then, after that to yourself, affirmation is to affirm but it is also actually taking responsibility for yourself as you are the Queen or King of yourself.

Prayer is part of this as it is a form of meditation. When I ask God to guide me to what I desire and I believe in God and have faith in only Him, as He is the Almighty and it is not in the hands of any human. He does not have favourites or bias and so it is possible to receive in reality through asking. Self-development has brought me closer to God because God only wants us to be satisfied and live in abundance and prosperity.

My religion is part of me and I do not need to hide anymore and when questioned, I do say that yes there's always something to be forgiven for and also when you need the guidance as He will always be there for you.

I had to read the names of God to remind myself of how powerful God is not just about the wrong you do and what punishment you will get as a result as God says when you ask for forgiveness, He is;- the all- merciful, the forgiving, the pure one, the source of peace, the guardian, the creator, the shaper of beauty, the giver of all, the reliever, the forgiver and hider of faults, the loving one and many more and that made me connected to God more than ever. Now that I am fully in surrender. When it comes to everything, I want I know that only by God's will, will I achieve everything and more. In my opinion, that comes down to believing in the Law of Attraction; as it goes hand in hand with my religion and I have watched as the pieces of a puzzle fitted together perfectly.

I have been born with fire in my belly; full of desires and dreams. I saw myself as different to everyone else as I saw women and young people suffering or being treated cruelly. That was my only weakness or is it my strength. This because it has made me who I am today. It helped me to empower people from a young age. By seeing life differently from others and when it comes to material things and richness it meant I was not swayed by them. As for me the most important thing to me is seeing people genuinely happy and giving love and care from myself to others.

I always believe and know that everything starts with a simple thought. If you think about one thing and really focus on it, you will turn it in to reality. It does not matter where you are from or what you are, it matters how you were conditioned from the time you are born to where you are now.

Remember to check if you are going through either one or all of these symptoms: Limiting Beliefs, Procrastination and Fear!!!

Limiting Beliefs:

Limiting Beliefs starts from the time you are young when you are helpless or vulnerable and, in a place, where you have no control over a situation or your own fate at such a young age.

These are some of the ideas that may affect some who are going through Limiting Beliefs. People may have treated you badly, bullied you, isolated you. Limiting Beliefs are often about ourselves and our self-identity. The beliefs may also be about other people and the world in general and that comes in to play a lot more when we are older. As we define ourselves by what we do or not do, we often have a limiting self-image, as we are bound by values, laws, cultures and religion. A belief system often plays a major factor in our lives and that is the one thing you will need to work on for the rest of your life.

Procrastination happens when we either do not believe in what we want for ourselves or the fear is holding us back. We are born with two fears and growing up we collect more fears from what we see and hear and are told by others around us or we create our own fear from anxiety, paranoia, stress and other environment threats.

We started from a sperm that won the race to the egg and we became children and survived childhood and then we went on to become adults.

And yes; some things have happened to you or yes sometimes you went through ordeals. But you survived and you are still here. Ask yourself now who in this world can stop you who you want to be, we have the best gift that we are given from god, or universe.

If you believe in God, the Universe or the Almighty; whatever you call the one who created you and everything around you. You were given this amazing gift and what is that gift; that is your mind? Your mind can take, learn and adapt to any situation given to mankind.

Our imagination can expand and stretch. All you need is to have an open mind and decide what you want to do and focus on it to create a greater you.

Challenge and task for you

This might help you to know what area of your life needs your attention, the wheel of life below is to be used by putting a dot on the level of where you are in your present moment. Put the dot at the top if all is great, put the dot in the middle if there is still room to grow and put the dot at the bottom if it is on the low end of your scale at this moment in your life.

You can write down or draw your own wheel of life on your journal and you will see every three months to six months and yearly how you progress and see how the shape of your life changes every time.

Wheel of life Image:

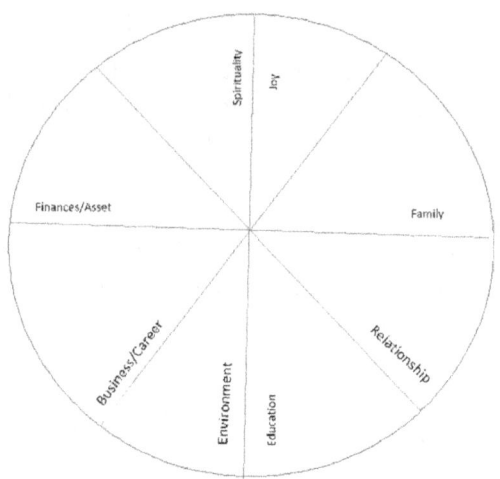

This Wheel of life will help you to identify where else in your life that you need to focus on. Now that you have gone through the work in order to find yourself and now you are ready to take more steps in what is surrounding you. I can imagine that you have grown so much now that whatever was holding you back before it will no longer seem a problem now.

It is alright if you want to take slower steps to ensure your success and we know there is still more work to do. I will explain more about your emotions and how it will help you or even motivate you to get the results you want in your life.

The first time I did the wheel of life it actually made me worried as I drew an island and I got overwhelmed. I did not understand that most of all these aspects of our lives are connected and the biggest challenge is that by working on our self that it will make it easier for everything else to flow in to place. With that said it does not mean you will be immune to personal disasters or challenges, but have the knowledge that you can overcome them by having more of a strategic plan and then have a successful lifestyle of your choice.

The wheel of life is your life map and it is there to measure your progress. It also shows you the blind spots for you to ensure your success is key in all areas of your life.

To use the wheel of life effectively use it every three months and evaluate it again in six months and then again in 12 months and you will see your progress and achieve everything you always wanted to achieve and more.

CHAPTER 14
CONFIDENCE IS THE NEW SEXY

"Instead of resisting any emotion, the best way to dispel it is to enter it fully, embrace it and see through your resistance."

-Deepak Chopra

Universally human beings experience emotions and this happens in three forms, 1- Thoughts 2- Habit and 3- Action.

This occurs in two different ways:

- ▶ Anxiety- to recognise Internal Threat
- ▶ Stress- an actual threat External

Anxiety and Stress prevents the same symptoms but differ because. anxiety is an internal, recognise internal threat whereas stress is external – concerning the surrounding pressures on you. This can now lead to mental illnesses if you do not look after yourself. In order to prevent you, you need to have an awareness of your thoughts, habits and actions.

Challenge and task for you

Please write down in your journal.

List how anxiety may affect you in the following ways:

1, thoughts 2, behaviour/habit 3, physical

Example of my own list below:

Some of my own list on how anxiety affects me;

Thoughts

- ▶ I have failed
- ▶ Heightened alertness
- ▶ Over thinking

Behaviour/habits

- ▶ Focused
- ▶ Driven
- ▶ Sleeping more or less

Physical

- ▶ Abdominal discomfort
- ▶ Headache

▶ Increased desire to defecate or urinate

Understanding what triggers your anxiety and the source of your stress within your life which will enable you to list what factors are in your life that help reduce and tackle your anxiety.

Some of my own list that helped me to reduce my anxiety;

▶ Note When I put myself down

▶ Being creative- make or play something

▶ Arrange future events, daily and special occasions.

▶ Socialise with family and friends

▶ Meditation

▶ Pray

▶ Sleep

▶ Feeling ok to say No

Key messages:

▶ The human psyche also consists of the emotional distress you suffer.

▶ This is a normal part of the human experience where the habits thoughts and feelings concerning your Emotional Distress are always affecting you. This can cause us to be unable to express our distress without being aggressive.

▶ Attempting to tackle this behaviour we employ differing techniques to deal with our emotional distress, acting as 'solutions' to the way we feel.

▶ Analysing the situation from an objective point of view

will allow you to understand different ways to deal with your emotional distress.

This book has explained some of these emotions we have and how we use them. When you look at the drawing below it will show you how important it is to have self-awareness. It is key to ensure you have a balanced and healthy lifestyle. The best way to be aware and to know your emotions is by measuring them on the scale of how you feel.

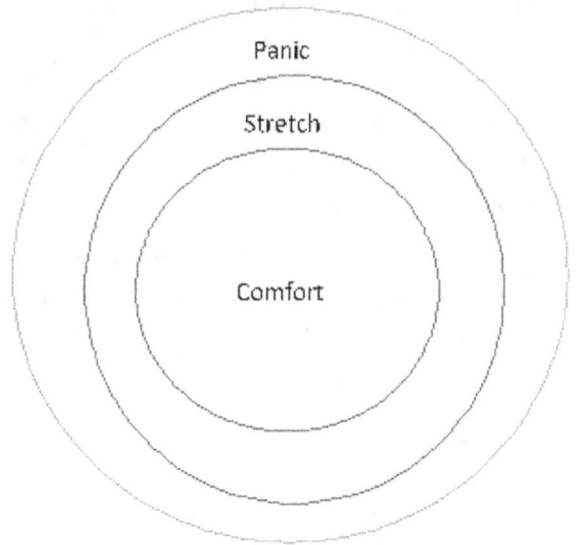

The middle part is Comfort, comfort is where you are safe but not growing on every part of our life we do find a place where we become safe and comfortable but when it comes to making a difference in our lives we can either go into panic mode or stretch when you have awareness to your emotions.

When you see and feel that you are experiencing panic when you do something, around people or in a group, in a certain environment or on a mode of transport. Ask yourself if you need the people or group of people and what is it that we receive from them that is worthy of your panic. If it is something that you do at work, home or to yourself ask yourself are you actually gaining or losing?

The way some of you who are reading this book; you might say that life is not black and white or good and bad or as simple as I am making it to be. You might be thinking that it can be like that for everyone else and that is alright. Like I said before from the beginning of this book, we are given a gift and that is freedom. Your life can be as easy as I put it; if you want to make it and choose it yourself. It is possible to have greatness and happiness and to be fully content with everything this life has to give. So, make it as simple as you can by choosing good vs not so good, love vs hate, empower vs disempower and many more.

This book is about having a relationship with yourself, knowing what works for you and what you want to improve in your life for the better. Looking after you is the first and most important step is to know the real you!!!

Boundaries:

Having clear boundaries is essential to a healthy, balanced lifestyle as it is essential in knowing who you are and what is not working for you. Learning about your boundaries can start with the little things like having awareness on your emotions. What or who makes us happy and what or who makes us unhappy? To choose what emotions are worth in our life over and over again and that can be either positive or negative.

Choosing Positive rather than Negative gives freedom after being hurt or wounded over and over again to the point you say "No more". That is about knowing your boundaries. It can even be as simple as having a choice of sweet or savoury; knowing what it is your taste buds desire! It is time to take away everything that is holding or chaining you down. Shred away what is not working within or standing in your way.

This is the time to say thank you to your past for teaching you and offering the strength it gave you, but now it is time to fully surrender to your new, clean, worthy, deserving full abundance. It begins with cleaning your slate and awakening your true potential.

Heart:

Your heart is where your power resides, your heart is melted by love and kindness and that is how you will manifest anything you ever want or desire.

As long as you know what you want then shift your focus away from the way you think about it to the way you feel about it and then put it into action. Remember this is about taking a leap and that needs to be a step by step approach not 10 steps at a time.

When you use your mind and heart combined together you will create wholeness in your life. By using it for peace, love, happiness and freedom continually raise your vibration you will receive your full abundance and that comes when you make time for you to still your mind and connect within to the source.

Be yourself at all times whether it is good, bad or ugly; as you are the person you must be real with. Accept yourself for who you are and be proud of the person you present to the world as this is only the beginning. The next step is letting the right people into your life who really deserve you for who you are no matter what.

Challenge and task for you

Write in your journal and every month revisit it.

- ▶ What do you desire or want?
- ▶ Create your own vision board
- ▶ Date your goals and write down everything you expect after you got your goals or desire,
- ▶ Who would you be as a person?
- ▶ What is the feeling you want to feel?
- ▶ Where would you be in the environment?

"You are always with yourself, so you might as well enjoy the company."

-Diane Von Furstenbe.

"life, she realized, so often become a determined, relentless avoidance of pain-of one's own, of other peoples. But sometimes pain had to be acknowledged and even touched so that one could move into it and through it and past it. Or else be destroyed by it."

-Mary Balogh

"As human beings we all want to be happy and free from misery... we have learned that the key to happiness is inner peace. The greatest obstacles to inner peace are disturbing emotions such as anger, attachment, fear and suspicion, while love and compassion and a sense of universal responsibility are the sources of peace and happiness."

-Dalai Lama

Love, Peace and Harmony.

With Love,

Barke Faraj

www.ingramcontent.com/pod-product-compliance
Lightning Source LLC
Chambersburg PA
CBHW071456070526
44578CB00001B/366